THE TROJAN WAR

BERNARD EVSLIN

Illustrated by William Hunter

SCHOLASTIC INC.
New York Toronto London Auckland Sydney

ISBN 0-590-41626-X

24 23 22 21 20 19 18 17   8 9/9 0/0

Printed in the U.S.A.   40

CONTENTS

THE PEDDLER

The man stooped under a huge bale. He passed through the castle gates and climbed the broad stone stairs that led to the women's quarters. The brass-helmeted sentries stood silently watching him go. Ordinarily they did a little playful torturing of peddlers before allowing them in — beat them a bit about the shoulders with their spear-shafts, plucked their beards, and scattered their wares. They weren't really cruel, these sentries, they were fighting men, but it had been a long time between wars, and they were bored. For some reason they had not bothered this red-headed fellow. Perhaps it was that his shoulders were so broad and his arms so knotted with muscle — and he had lifted the great bale of goods so easily off his white donkey. His grin was servile enough, and he had tipped them a greasy little bow like all peddlers. Nevertheless, they let him pass through the gates and across the courtyard without tormenting him.

And it was strange, too, that the great guard dogs, the brindle mastiffs with their spiked brass collars, did not charge the stranger, nor even growl.

The peddler flung down his bale and knelt on the stone-flagged floor, pulling out garment after shining garment as the tall daughters of King Scyros crowded about him, chattering and laughing and shrieking with greed. For they loved clothes, these daughters of the king, and Scyros was such a remote island, they felt themselves falling far behind the fashions. Besides . . . they had a visitor to impress: the tall yellow-headed silent girl — a country cousin who had been with them for three months now without ever telling them anything about herself. She listened to all they had to say, smiling her curious thin-lipped smile, but never told any secrets in return.

"Spread out your wares, man," cried Calyx, the eldest princess. "Don't pull them out one by one. Spread them so we can see them all."

"Yes, princess," said the peddler.

With a sweep of his arm he spread his goods upon the stone floor. Silks and furs and garments of wonderfully woven flax, dyed with the colors of mountain sunset. Jewels flashed — rings, bracelets, anklets, necklaces. And, on a long cloak of black wool, were couched a lance and a sword. Unjewelled were these weapons, made for battle use not ceremony; their blades were heavy and sharp, newly honed. The hilt of the sword was bull-horn; the haft of the throwing lance of polished ash, its head of bronze. With gull-cries of greed the girls fell upon the garments — all except their visitor. She leaped across the chamber and snatched up the weapons. Flexed her long legs in a fighting stance, and whipped the sword through the air, decapitating a horde of imaginary foes.

6

The princesses fell silent, stared at their cousin, eyes huge. The peddler smiled. He arose. His stoop was gone, gone the little servile selling-grin. He stood there massively, smiling, and watched as the princesses' yellow-headed cousin shadow-duelled — whirling, ducking, stabbing.

"It is well," said the peddler. And his voice was different too. "By your choices shall you be known. I have come a long way for you, Achilles. And now you must come back with me."

"Achilles!" shrieked the maidens.

"Achilles," said the peddler.

He approached the tall girl, seized the shoulder of her tunic, and ripped it away, baring her to the waist, and disclosing not another maiden, but a young man muscled like the statue of a god.

"A man," murmured the princesses. "She's a man."

The young man said nothing, but seized the peddler by the beard and raised his sword.

"Softly, Achilles," said the peddler. "I too am unlike what I seem. We are kinsmen far back, you and I. I am Ulysses, King of Ithaca."

"Ulysses? You?"

Achilles let his hand fall.

"Ulysses," echoed the princesses.

And, indeed, even before the Trojan War was fought this name was known the length and breadth of Hellas as that of the boldest pirate-king of the Inner Sea, a master of strategy on land and water.

"But why do you seek me, cousin?" said Achilles. "My mother bade me dress in maiden's garb and hide myself in this court in obedience to some oracle or other. She said she would call me back when the Fates had been satisfied — a matter of weeks. But now you come first to fetch me away. By what right?"

"Oh, you may abide here among the maidens and wait for your mother," said Ulysses. "But I think I should tell you that there's a war on."

"A war?" shouted Achilles, snatching up his sword. "A real war?"

"Very real. With Troy. Against some of the most fearsome warriors of this age or any other."

"Why do we stand here conversing?" cried Achilles. "Let's go!"

Ulysses bowed to the princesses. "You may keep these garments, fair maidens. They are my gift to you. Accept too my apologies for the slight deceit I was forced to practice."

"Farewell, cousins," said Achilles. "Gentle maids, farewell. After this war is over, I shall return — in my own guise, and attempt to thank you for your hospitality."

The two men passed from the chamber, and left the courtyard. The princesses watched from the embrasures; saw them disappear through the gates and then appear again around the corner of the cliff where the road dipped to the sea. And that night nine of them dreamed of Achilles, and three, of Ulysses. But in the middle darkness their dreams crossed, and by dawn there was no counting.

Ulysses led the young man aboard his ship. They lifted anchor and set sail for Aulis where the war fleet was gathering. They sat on deck in the golden weather, and Ulysses told of how enmity was born between Greece and Troy.

SEEDS OF WAR

"Actually, you and this war were meant for each other," he said to Achilles. "Your seeds were planted on the same night — the night your mother and father were wed — at a wedding feast given by the gods themselves on Mt. Olympus. Know you, Achilles, that your father, Peleus, was the most renowned warrior of his day, and your mother, Thetis, the most beautiful naiad who ever rose naked and dripping from the tides of the moon to trouble man's sleep?"

"I'm aware of my own pedigree, man," snapped Achilles. "Get to the war."

"Patience, young friend, the war comes soon enough. Now, whoever it was of the High Ones who made out the invitation list to the wedding feast, neglected to include the Lady of Discord herself. Eris, queen of Harpies, sister to the War-god, who rides beside him in his chariot delighting in the cries of the wounded and the smell of blood, was not invited to the feast and, oh, Achilles, what a terrible omission it was.

"When the rejoicing was at its height and the stars reeled on their crystal axes, shaken by the laughter of the gods, then it was that Eris made herself invisible, entered the great banquet hall, and rolled upon the table a gleaming, heavy apple of solid gold. Upon the apple were written the words: 'To the most beautiful.' It glowed there like the heart of flame, and was immediately claimed by Hera, Athena, and Aphrodite. The festivities were immediately rent by their quarreling as they shrieked like fishwives over a beached mackerel. The feast was ruined. Gentle Hestia, Goddess of the Hearth, and protector of feasts, wept great tears. Eris stood among the shadows, chuckling. Hestia begged Zeus to settle things by awarding the apple to whoever he considered to be the most beautiful. But Father Zeus was much too wise to be caught in a trap like that. Hera happened to be his sister and his wife, Athena his daughter, and Aphrodite a kind of half-sister — and, it is said, even more.

" 'Peace, good company!' boomed Zeus. 'The question of choosing among three such enchanting beauties is too difficult to be undertaken by anyone who knows them well and has been exposed to their potent charms. We must therefore seek beyond our own small circle for a just decision. I shall search among the mortals of the earth for him of coolest judgment and most exquisite taste. Give me a few days to find him. In the meantime, I bid you cease your quarreling, my three fair claimants, and let the festivities resume. As for this little gem of contention, I shall just keep it myself until judgment is made.' And his huge hand closed lovingly about the golden apple."

"The war, man! The war!" cried Achilles. "Enough of parents, weddings, and high vanities! When will your tale tell of war?"

"Hark, now. These events I relate are the living seeds, and they will bear bloody fruit, I promise. And you, my boy, will be there for the harvesting. Where was I?"

"Zeus was seeking one wise among mortals to give judgment upon the claims of the goddesses."

"He chose Paris. Paris, secret prince of Troy, Priam's youngest son, thought to have been killed at birth because an oracle had warned that his deeds would destroy Troy."

"Reason enough for the king to drown him like a kitten. How is it he survived?"

"Oh, some plot of Hecuba's, no doubt. A mother's heart cherishes her sons, even those who endanger the state. It is said Queen Hecuba instructed her serving man to smuggle the babe out of the castle and give it to a certain shepherd to raise as his own. He grew up to be very beautiful. It's a handsome family anyway, and he is the fairest by far, they say, of Priam's fifty sons. The shepherd maids trailed him up and down the slopes. But he was too young; he spurned the maidens. And this, of course, recommended him to uneasy husbands and lovers, giving them a great opinion of his wisdom and moderation. So it was that he was called upon to mediate their disputes, to fix grazing rights, judge the points of cattle, and so forth. When Zeus bent his ear to earth to hear of a man of judgment, why the strongest word came from Mt. Ida, speaking the name, Paris. . . ."

The hot silver of a flying fish scudded suddenly out of the water followed by the black-silver hump of a broaching dolphin. For half a breath they hung in the air — long enough for Achilles to uncoil from the deck with a fluency that delighted the warrior heart of Ulysses. Swiftly, Achilles hurled a short lance through the air transfixing the winged fish so that it fell heavily before the dolphin — which drew out the lance, swam to the boat, and tossed the weapon aboard with a flick of its

11

head, grinning up at the men like a dog. Then it turned and swam back for its meal.

"Well thrown," said Ulysses.

"It thirsts for blood," said Achilles, wiping his lance-head. "I must appease it with hunting till it can drink of the enemy upon the beaches of Troy. Unless, of course, I am lucky enough to fall in with a private quarrel."

"Strictly forbidden," said Ulysses. "There's a war on. Private quarrels must wait. We have all taken an oath, and you must too."

"Tell the tale, King of Ithaca. It shortens the journey."

THE JUDGMENT OF PARIS

They were fighting a headwind out of Scyros, and Ulysses saw that it would take some days to reach Aulis. So he told the story in the old bardic way with many a trill and flourish, and taking every byroad. But we will shorten it. . . .

In those days it was customary to bribe judges, which shows how far we have come since. And so Paris was offered bribes.

Hera offered him power. "Great fleets shall sail at your nod," she told him. "Armies shall march when you raise your hand. Dominion shall be yours over land and sea. All men shall be as slaves to you. Your smile will quicken them, your frown kill.

And power is wealth. Your slaves will delve the earth for gold and jewels. Your galleys will plunder far places and sail back with cargoes beyond dreams of piracy to stuff your vaults. All this shall be yours if you award me the apple.

"Reverence, you will agree, is the highest wisdom. How can you judge more wisely than by conforming to the judgment of Father Zeus, master of choices, who of all living creatures chose me, me, me as his wife? A more serious choice, you understand, than among you mortals, for neither of us can die and he must keep me to wife through all eternity.

"Be reverent then, Paris. Be rich and powerful. Choose me, Hera. Let the apple be mine."

Athena spoke next. "Father Zeus, remember, has appointed you judge, meaning that he throws his own divine power behind your judgment. Otherwise he would have judged for himself. As for Hera's argument, it signifies nothing. Anyone acquainted with affairs on Olympus knows that it is godly to keep titles within the immediate family — that is the only reason Zeus married his sister. And it has been amply proved that he finds others more attractive than his wife.

"As for her offer, I can overbid that too. I offer you wisdom. Born from Zeus' head, I am Patroness of Intellectual Activities, you know, and wisdom is uniquely mine to offer. And without wisdom power loses its potence and wealth grows poor. I can teach you to know, to penetrate the innermost secrets of man's soul, and disclose to you certain divine secrets which men call nature. With such knowledge you will have mastery over other men and, more important, mastery over yourself. As for Hera's glittering promises, remember this: I am also Mistress of Strategy. Before battle, captains pray to me for tactics. Give me that apple and I will make you the greatest soldier of the age — and everyone knows that power and wealth depend finally on victory in war. Be wise, Paris, choose the Goddess of Wisdom."

All Aphrodite said was: "Come closer . . ."

When he approached, she touched him, and the world changed. The sun dived into the sea and made it boil, and his blood boiled too. He felt himself going red-hot like a poker in the fire. Then she touched him with her other hand and a delicious icy coolness washed over him. He forgot everything but the touch of her hands, her fragrance, the music of her voice, saying:

"I am Aphrodite, Goddess of Love. I give you the first of two gifts now, and ask no promise. This gift is your own body, instrument of pleasure, wherein is contained the only true wealth, the only true power, the only wisdom. You shall receive the second gift after you have delivered judgment. There is a mortal woman on earth said to rival me in beauty. She is Helen, Queen of Sparta, and I hereby promise her to you."

Without hesitation, Paris awarded the apple to Aphrodite.

Screaming like Harpies, Athena and Hera flew back to Olympus and flung themselves before Zeus, trying to get Aphrodite disqualified for illegal use of hands. But Zeus laughed at them. He agreed with Paris' choice, and was thankful that it would be the young shepherd prince, and not himself, who would attract the savage reprisals of the goddesses.

Aflame with Aphrodite's touch, drunk with her promise, Paris dropped his role of shepherd and returned to Troy. He stormed into the great throne-room and swept the astounded Priam and Hecuba into his embrace, demanding they recognize him as their son. All their hesitations and fears were burned away in the blaze of his beauty, and they received him with great joy. His forty-nine brothers were a bit more dubious, remembering what the oracle had warned, but Priam was king and his wish was law. Besides, things had been dull and peaceful for some time and the prospect of danger was not unwelcome.

Then Paris asked that a ship be fitted out so that he might make an embassy to the kingdom of Sparta.

"I can tell you no more, Venerable Majesty. I must speak no further, brothers. The purpose of my voyage is a secret between me and the gods. But I promise you this: When I return I shall bring with me a cargo such as no ship has ever carried — and

15

with it undying fame for us all. Thus a goddess has assured me in secret, and that secret is my destiny."

A small fleet was fitted out, and Paris sailed away for Sparta. In a few weeks' time he returned, bringing Helen with him. There, before all Troy, he declared her his wife, admitting that she was encumbered with a prior husband, but considering this detail beneath consideration. When Menelaus came to Troy, as come he must, then he, Paris, would engage the husband in single combat, and with one thrust of his spear make Helen half a widow and wholly a wife.

Priam and Hecuba, and Paris' forty-nine brothers and fifty sisters fully understood what was happening: Paris had not only stolen another man's wife but, even worse, committed a breach of hospitality, a much more serious sacrilege. They knew Troy would shortly be plunged into a bloody war with the most powerful chieftains of Achaea, Helles, Boetia, Sparta, Athens, and that entire warlike peninsula not yet called Greece.

But when Helen smiled at them they forgot all their fears. "It's true," they whispered to each other. "She's as beautiful as Aphrodite. Surely the gods will allow us to protect such a treasure."

The only dissenting voice was that of Cassandra, Priam's youngest daughter. Apollo had wooed her one summer past. His sunstroke caress left her with visions; the future painted itself in smoky pictures for her to read. But she had tired of the sun-god's touch, and Apollo, maddened, had said:

"Wicked girl, you shall choke with frustration even as I do now. I have given you the gift of prophecy, and now I make that gift a punishment. The more accurate your prediction, the less you shall be believed. And the colder the disbelief, the more ardent your forecast."

Now, even as Paris introduced Helen to the court, and the tall lovers stood in a blaze of acceptance and love, with Priam's fifty sons beating their spear-shafts on their shields and bawling

16

defiance at the Greeks, even then Cassandra lifted her voice in prophecy:

"Hear me, Trojans, hear me. Return Helen; she brings death. Your fair city will be rent stone from stone, your young men slaughtered, your ancients shamed, and your women and children taken into slavery. Ship her back to Sparta before it is too late . . . too late . . . too late . . ."

Helen, hearing only her name spoken, smiled at the girl. And the crowd, seeing her smile, went wild with enthusiasm. Cassandra's words were heeded no more than if they had been the small wind rattling the leaves. The girl fell silent, moaning softly as the thwarted vision dug its fangs into her head.

"And that is why we're off to Troy now," said Ulysses to Achilles. "The events I have related to you, young falcon, are the roots of this war."

"All this to retrieve a runaway bride?" said Achilles. "One reason to fight is as good as another, so long as you fight, but I would have expected a great war to have a greater cause."

"You haven't seen the lady," said Ulysses.

"Oh, I understand what you tell me, that she's enough to send the Trojans mad. But then they're half-mad to begin with."

"I repeat, you haven't seen the lady, or you wouldn't talk like that. She's enough to send more than Trojans mad. She's maddened some very hard-headed Greeks that I know of . . . all of us, to be sure. We were all her suitors — every prince and chieftain of the Peloponnese and its islands — so many of us and such a fierce brawling crew that her foster father, Tyndareus, didn't dare give her to any one for fear he might offend the others. So he kept fobbing us off with one excuse after another until we were all ready to fly at each other's throats. Finally, I came up with a little plan: that each suitor take an oath to abide by Helen's own choice of husband and forbear from attacking the lucky man — or Tyndareus. Further, we would all swear to a binding alliance, so that if anyone else attacked her husband and attempted to rob him of Helen, we would band together and punish the interloper. We swore a most sacred oath on the quartered carcass of a horse. And that is why we must all go now to the aid of Menelaus, and pursue Paris even into Troy itself."

"Are they good fighters, the Trojans?" asked Achilles.

"The best — next to us. And, in their own minds, they have no such reservation. There will be keen fighting, never doubt it. We all wish to help Menelaus, of course, but each of us also sees something in it for himself. Fame. A chance to use our swords before they grow rusty. Also slaves. And mountains of loot. Troy is a very rich city, far richer than any of ours. And there is something else. The city stands upon a headland commanding the straits which lead into the Black Sea and to the rich land of Scythia, where there are boundless opportunities for trade and slave-raids, piracy, and other commercial traffic. But while Troy stands, our fleets can never enter those straits, nor can we penetrate the lands of the Black Sea nor the further mysterious reaches of Asia, whose east winds fairly reek of wealth. These are considerations too, lad."

"All I want to do is fight," said Achilles. "I'll leave the reasons to you."

"Well, you should get your stomachful. Our forces are to be led by Agamemnon, King of Mycenae, and brother to Menelaus. He is a bold, practical leader, very aggressive, very ruthless. He is married to Helen's elder sister, Clytemnestra, and so has a double motive for adopting his brother's blood-feud with the royal family of Troy."

What Ulysses did not tell Achilles was that he himself had tried a little draft-dodging before coming to Scyros. An oracle had said that if Ulysses went off to fight at Troy it would be twenty years before he could come home and, when he did so, it would be as a penniless vagabond, recognized by no one. So, when Agamemnon and Palamedes, King of Euboea, came to Ithaca to demand his aid against Troy, he tried to evade his

18

vow by feigning madness. He put on a tall, pointed fool's hat and harnessed a bull and a goat to his plow, sowing his furrow with salt instead of seed. But, after watching him for a bit, Palamedes, who was almost as crafty as Ulysses, decided to give him a sanity test. He plucked Ulysses' infant son from his nurse's arms and set him on the ground in the path of the oncoming plow. Ulysses reined his animals short, and snatched the babe out of danger.

"You're fit for fighting," said Palamedes. "Drop the bluff, and come along."

"A parent's instinct is stronger than reason — I mean unreason," said Ulysses. "But I assure you my wits are deranged."

"Nonsense," growled Agamemnon. "How sane do you have to be to make war? In this affair a touch of madness may help. You have the right sort of wits for us, Ulysses. So keep your oath, and come away."

THE
EVENTS
AT AULIS

They found a thousand ships at Aulis and the greatest gathering of heroes since the beginning of time. Their commander was Agamemnon, an angry bull of a man, burly as the stump of an oak, with a dark red face and eyes as cold and hard as chunks of lava — until he became enraged, when they glowed like hot coals. His voice of command was like the bellowing of a bull.

Now when Achilles smelled a fight his blood did not heat, nor did excitement take him. A delicious chill prickled over all his body, sweet cold airs wrapped themselves about his limbs, cool fingers stroked his hair, and in his mouth was a taste like honey. He fought with gleaming chest and flashing arm and marvellously thewed leg, and he smiled his lipless smile all the while. He did not shout, except when summoning his men, but uttered a low crooning sound like a love song. Men, fighting him, felt his blade at their throats like an act of deliverance.

Now when he saw the bull-man, Agamemnon, he felt that delicious chill touch his neck, and he knew that in all the world this man was his archenemy, even though they were fighting on the same side, and that his main problem in the war to come would be how to refrain from attacking his Commander.

And Agamemnon gazed at Achilles with no great favor when Ulysses led the young man over to present him.

"Hail, great Agamemnon," said Ulysses. "I wish you to meet Achilles, and to value him as I do. For, according to prophecy, it is his courage and skill that will bring us to victory in the war to come."

"Oracles take delight in riddling," said Agamemnon. "They never speak straight any more. I welcome you, young man, and look forward to seeing you display that courage and skill of which the oracle speaks."

"Thank you," said Achilles.

"The oracle holds also that you will not survive this war," said Agamemnon. "I suppose that is why your mother hid you away among the maidens of Scyros."

"I suppose so," said Achilles. "But you know how parents are. How devouring their love can be."

Ulysses snorted with laughter. The blood flamed in Agamemnon's face. This was a shrewd rejoinder of Achilles' relating to a scandal in Agamemnon's family. Agamemnon's father, Atreus, had committed one of the most unsavory crimes in history. He had butchered his nephews and served them up in a stew to their father, his brother, Tryestes, all so that he could seize the throne of Mycenae and rule unchallenged, the same throne that Agamemnon had inherited.

Ulysses eyed Agamemnon closely. He knew that the man

was seething with rage, and was only a hairbreadth from striking out at Achilles.

And he saw that Achilles, lightly balancing on the balls of his feet, ready to move in any direction, was smiling his little lipless smile.

But Agamemnon mastered himself, and said: "Truly, Achilles, if your sword is as sharp as your tongue you should do great damage to the Trojans. In the meantime — welcome. We shall converse again when your Myrmidons arrive. Then you may report for instructions about their quartering, forage for the horses, sailing order, and so forth."

"Very good, sir," said Achilles. "Thank you for your courtesy."

Thus, bloodshed was averted upon that first meeting. But the note of hatred struck between them was to devil the efforts of the Greeks and almost lead to their defeat.

Next, Ulysses took the young man about the encampment and introduced him to the other great chieftains. He met Palamedes, King of Euboea, most skilled artificer since Daedalus; and Diomedes, King of Argos, a man, it was said, who had never known fear. He was presented to the two warriors named Ajax. One was Ajax of Salamis, strongest mortal since Hercules, head and shoulders taller than Achilles. And again, the young man, measuring the giant with his eyes, felt a breath of that sweet combative chill. But he could work up no fighting wrath. For the huge man grinned down at him, and said: "Stop puffing your chest like a rooster. You and I are going to be friends, and fight only Trojans."

He clapped his great meaty paw on Achilles' shoulder — a blow hard enough to cripple an ordinary man. Achilles accepted it as a friendly tap, and nodded gravely back at Ajax.

Now all the tested warriors received the young man with marks of esteem even though he had not yet proved himself in battle. They had heard startling reports of him from his old tutor, Phoenix — a man much feared by foemen — who was there at Aulis as a member of the War Council. Phoenix had told how he had managed the education of the young Achilles. He had taken him and his elder cousin, Patroclus, onto the wild slopes of Mt. Pelion, Achilles being seven years old then, and Patroclus twelve. He had fed the younger boy on the bloody meat of courage itself, restricting his diet to the entrails of bear and wolf and lion, which Achilles had eaten greedily, but Patroclus had refused. He told how he had recruited the centaur, Cheiron, to help raise the boys, and how Cheiron had taught Achilles to run more swiftly than a staghound, how to hunt down the wild boar without the use of hounds, and to split a willow wand with his spear at a hundred yards.

Patroclus he had tutored in the softer arts, the use of herbs and music in healing, and how to play the pipe and psaltery. At the age of thirteen, Achilles had singlehandedly slaughtered a robber band that, for years, had terrified the villagers on Mt. Pelion. He had been wounded in thigh and shoulder in this fight, and Patroclus had tended him and nursed him back to health. With such tales had Phoenix stuffed the other leaders at Aulis, so it was little wonder they were ready to extend a hearty welcome to Achilles.

And the young warrior was overjoyed to meet his old tutor in this place, and was even happier to learn that his dear cousin and playmate, Patroclus, was sailing toward Aulis at the head of the Myrmidons.

THE SIEGE BEGINS

Ulysses had warned that the war would be a long one, but Agamemnon, who always preferred to believe what was most convenient, was confident of a quick victory. When the Greeks landed on the Trojan beaches they met stiff resistance. A Trojan hero, Cycnus — son of Poseidon — a man who could not be wounded by sword or spear, captained the beach party and fought like a demon, almost driving the Greeks into the sea. Achilles it was who finally killed him without weapon, by twisting Cycnus' helmet so that he was strangled by his own chinstrap.

Then the Greeks rallied and fought their way to the Trojan wall but met so savage a defense that they had to withdraw.

At the War Council, Ulysses said: "I was right, unfortunately.

It will be a long war. Their walls are huge, their men brave, and they have at least three magnificent warriors, Prince Hector, his young brother Troilus, and his cousin Aeneas. Sheltered by such walls, led by such heroes, they are too powerful for direct assault. We shall have to lay siege. But in the meantime, by using our sea-power, we can raid the nearby islands one by one. This will strip Troy of her allies, and provide us with food and slaves."

It was agreed, and Achilles was named commander of the raiding parties. During the next eight years he attacked the home islands of Troy's allies one by one, sacked their cities and took much loot and many slaves. All this time the main body of the Greeks encamped on the beach behind a stockade of pointed stakes and laid siege to the mighty city.

But a siege is a tedious business, and quarrels flared among the men who had grown tired of the war and longed for home. The bitterest squabbles were provoked by the division of slaves. One of these almost sent the Greeks home in defeat.

THE QUARREL

On one raid Achilles captured Cressida, one of the loveliest young maidens of Troy. She was a smoky-eyed, honey-skinned girl with a low hoarse voice. When Agamemnon heard her speak at the Dividing of the Spoils he felt her voice running over the nerve-ends of his face, like a cat's tongue licking him. He immediately claimed her as his share of the booty. Ordinarily, Achilles would have disputed this claim, and an ugly squabble would have flared, but upon this raid Achilles had captured a girl he fancied even more, a tall green-eyed maiden named Briseis. So Agamemnon's claim was allowed and he took Cressida for his slave. She was hard to handle at first, but Agamemnon had a way with girls and soon she was content.

But her father was not happy. His name was Chryse; he was a priest of Apollo, and a soothsayer. He came under a truce to Agamemnon's tent and begged the release of his daughter, offering a generous ransom. But Agamemnon would have none of it. He drove her father away with harsh words. The old man, furious and humiliated, prayed to Apollo as he hobbled back toward Troy.

"Oh, Phoebus, I implore you, curb that haughty spirit. Punish Agamemnon, who keeps my daughter in vile servitude. Today he insults your servant, Apollo, tomorrow he will insult your holy self. For he is a most arrogant Greek, overbearing and imperious, ready to affront a god should his will be questioned."

It suited Apollo to hear this prayer. He favored the Trojans in the war, and felt it was time to do the Greeks a mischief. So he descended that night and stood between the great wall and the Greek encampment on the beach. He shot arrows of pestilence among the tents. They were tipped with fever; they ignited the camp refuse; foul vapors caught fire. Again and again Apollo shot his arrows. Where they struck, plague burned. Man and beast sickened. In the morning they awoke to die. Horses died, and cattle. In three days the Greeks had lost half as many troops as they had in nine years of fighting.

Ulysses urged Agamemnon to call a council. The oracle, Calchas, was consulted — because it was known that plague is sent by the gods in punishment for some affront, real or fancied, and it is always necessary to find out which god, so that the insult might be undone. But Calchas balked when he was called upon for interpretation.

"Pardon, great king," he said to Agamemnon. "But I would far rather you called upon another oracle."

"Why should we?" said Ulysses. "You're the best we have, and the best is what we need."

Agamemnon said: "Read the signs, O Calchas, and tell us true."

"I have read the signs. And the truth will anger you. And who will protect me from your sudden wrath?"

"I will," said Achilles, looking at Agamemnon. "I guarantee your safety."

"Hear then the reason for this pestilence. Our high king and war-leader, Agamemnon, has angered Apollo by insulting his priest, Chryse, who seeks the return of his daughter, Cressida. Agamemnon's angry refusal has kindled the radiant wrath of Phoebus who descended with a quiverful of plague darts which he flung into our tents so that we sicken and die."

"I don't believe it," roared Agamemnon.

"It makes sense," Achilles said. "Speak on, Calchas. Tell us how we can placate Apollo and avert this plague."

"The remedy is obvious," said Calchas. "Cressida must be returned to her father, without ransom. Then a clean wind will spring from the sea blowing away the pestilence."

Agamemnon turned savagely upon Calchas.

"You miserable, spiteful, croaking old raven. You have never yet in all the years I have known you spoke me a favorable auspice. Whether studying the flight of birds, examining their entrails, or casting bones, by whatever secret contrivance you read the riddle of the future, it is always to my disadvantage. In your eyes I am always angering the gods, as if they had nothing to do but perch on Olympus watching me night and day and seeking cause for anger in the actions of this one poor mortal, while they ignore everyone else on earth.

"At Aulis you said I had angered Artemis by not invoking her aid in some hunt or other, and that it was she who had sent the northeast gale to keep us penned in the harbor and prevent our fleet from sailing for Troy. And it was not until you prevailed upon me to sacrifice my own eldest, dearest daughter, Iphigenia, that you were satisfied. And now . . . now . . . you wish to rob me of even a greater prize, the smoky-eyed

Cressida, so much more beautiful and skillful than my own wife, Clytemnestra. Now you seek to rob me of the one prize I value after nine years of bloody toil on these beaches, bidding me tear my very heart from my body to appease Apollo. And the Royal Council agrees with you. The Chiefs agree with you. Very well, so be it. But, by the easily angered Gods, know this: I will not be left without a prize. If you take Cressida from me, I will take someone else's beautiful and clever slave girl."

Achilles sprang to his feet. "And from what common pen of slaves do you expect to draw your compensation?" he cried. "In your blind and matchless greed you have forgotten that each man takes his own prize as divided according to your own unjust decrees — whereby you always get the lion's share . . . or should I say the swine's share? No, you must give up Cressida without immediate compensation. For no man here, I believe, will give up what is his own. But when we raid another rich colony, or when Troy itself finally falls, if ever it does, then you will be able to take booty that will glut even your greed."

"You are a mighty warrior, Achilles," said Agamemnon. "But your spear speaks more surely than your tongue. I am High King, chosen by all of you in a choice certified by the gods. To deprive me of any jot or iota of my rights is sacrilege. Not only foolish, but impious. It is my duty to take someone else's slave to repay me for the loss of the lovely Cressida. For a king deprived is half a king, and half a king means defeat in warfare. If I want your slave, Achilles, or Ulysses', or one of Diomedes', or any creature I choose, all I have to do is reach my hand and take. But that will all be decided later. For the moment I consent. Cressida shall be returned so that the plague may end."

"Why you great snorting hog!" cried Achilles. "You are more fit to king it over a pigpen somewhere than to try to lead a band of free men. So this is how you would arrange things — that the burden should fall always on me, while you grab the spoils for yourself. Well, I've had enough. I'm tired of fighting your battles, and those of your brother who wasn't man enough to keep his wife at home. I'm taking my Myrmidons and sailing away. And we will see how you make out against Hector and his brothers."

"Go where you will, you bragging brawler," said Agamemnon. "You're better at fighting friends than enemies anyway. Board your beaked ship and sail where you will — to Hades I hope. But I swear by my crown that when you go you shall leave Briseis behind. And I shall take her to replace Cressida."

Now the lion wrath of Achilles rose in his breast and choked him with its sulphurous bile. He could think of nothing but to kill Agamemnon where he stood. He drew his sword, but a strong hand caught his arm. It was Athena, heaven-descended, invisible to everyone but Achilles. She fixed him with eyes so brilliant that they seemed to scorch his face. An unearthly musk came off her white arms. But Achilles was too angry to be intimidated.

"Great goddess," he said. "I love and venerate you. But if you have come to stop me from killing Agamemnon you are wasting your time. He has insulted me and must pay with his life."

"Where life and death are concerned," said Athena, "only the gods say 'must.' You are the greatest of mortals, Achilles, but I have come to tell you this! You are not to kill Agamemnon. Hera, Queen of the Gods, and I myself, are mightily interested in the victory of Greek arms. We can allow no squabbling among your leaders, no division among your troops. As for your wrath, it is justified, and I promise you this: Within a space of days, great Agamemnon will humble himself to you and offer the return of your slave girl and gifts more valuable than you can reckon. I promise you this. Hera promises it. But you must obey us."

'I listen and obey," said Achilles. "I will hold my hand from him, and he shall live — at least until the next time. But I shall never fight under his leadership again."

"Yes . . . tell him so," said Athena. "Attack him in words as fiercely as you will. For the man has been blinded by greed to the detriment of his leadership, and he must be shaken up, or victory will elude you Greeks whom the best gods love. Tell him what you will, say what you will, but do not kill him."

Athena disappeared. Achilles sheathed his sword again, saying: "You are a putrid cur, Agamemnon, unfit to lead men in battle. Only by the grace of heaven am I sparing your life now. But I shall not follow your example and squabble over a slave girl. Take her if you must, you besotted swine. But I tell you this. I will not fight against Troy. I will not contend against Hector and his brothers. Priam's brave sons and the Trojan troops shall go unchecked for all of me. From now on I pay no heed to battle, but fit out my ships for the voyage home. And when Hector is winnowing your ranks like the man with the scythe among the September wheat — yes, when you see your troops falling by the dozens before that terrible sword — then, then will you eat out your heart in remorse for having treated Achilles so."

Achilles stalked off, leaving the Council aghast.

THETIS

                         Before the Council broke up, the ancient general, Nestor, who had led three generations of warriors, and was now Agamemnon's most trusted adviser, addressed the assembly. He tried to dissuade Agamemnon from the path he had chosen. But though the eloquence flowed sweet as nectar from his mouth, the high king could not be swayed. He sent two messengers to Achilles' tent to bear away the beautiful Briseis. And Achilles watched them take the girl and did not offer them harm, although they trembled at his shadow. But he was too fair-minded to blame Agamemnon's messengers for the king's own evil, and he was forced to hold his hand from Agamemnon because of Athena's command. But he wept as he saw Briseis being borne off. He turned to face the sea.

"O deep mother," he prayed. "Thetis of the Silver Feet — you who rise from the tides of the moon to trouble man's sleep forever — you who led my father a chase through all the changes of beast and fish before you allowed yourself to be caught . . . you, Thetis, my mother, most beautiful and generous of naiads, help me now. Or I shall strangle here of a choler I cannot lance with my good blade."

Thetis was sporting then in the depths of the sea, fleeing Poseidon, allowing him almost to catch her, then escaping his attentions by dodging behind a giant squid, which she tickled, making the great jellied creature cast a curtain of black ink between her and her pursuer. In the midst of her sport her son's voice drifted down to her, and she arose from the sea like a mist.

"Oh, my brave son," she cried. "Why these tears? Tell your mother so that she may share your grief."

"Welcome, gentle mother," said Achilles. "Thank you for coming when I call. I suffer thus because Agamemnon, the High King, has offered me ignoble insult. Denied by the gods of his own slave girl, he has taken my beautiful Briseis, into his tent. And I am forbidden by Athena to draw my sword from its sheath, but must stand helplessly by and watch myself despoiled."

"Ever-meddlesome Athena!" cried Thetis. "Powerful you are, but I have powers too."

"Yes, mother, the owl-goddess has forbidden me vengeance. I must stand here choking back my wrath and, oh, mother, it is too bitter to swallow."

"What would you have me do, my son? How can I help you?"

"You must intercede with father Zeus whose edict overbears Athena's, and all the gods'. Speak winningly to him, mother, as you alone can do. Warm his interest in my behalf. Let him nod toward Troy, infusing courage into the Trojan hearts, and

33

strength into the Trojan arms. Let haughty Agamemnon find himself penned on the beaches while swift Hector and his brothers slaughter the Achaean forces. Then, then, will he rend his beard and weep for Achilles."

"I shall do so," said Thetis. "Swiftly will I travel to the Bronze Palace of the All-High, and beseech his intervention in your behalf. Those two mighty hags, Hera and Athena, keep close watch upon him, seeing that he does not intercede for Troy. But he still has some measure of regard for me, no doubt, and I still own some powers of persuasion, I am told. So rest easy, son. Wrap yourself in your cloak and taste sweet dreamless repose as your mother does your bidding. And gladly will she do it. For, in truth, you are the loveliest, strongest son that any mother, mortal or goddess, was blessed with."

She disappeared into the sea. Achilles lay down and went to sleep and did not dream.

Upon that same night Cressida was returned to her father.

Now, like a great white sea-bird, silver-footed Thetis flew to the Bronze Palace of Zeus, high on Mt. Olympus. She found him seated on a throne of black rock in his garden looking down upon the earth. He smiled when he saw her for she had long been a favorite of his. Then, remembering that Hera might be watching, his smile quickly changed to a frown. But Thetis had felt the first warmth of his smile, a warmth that melted snow out of season in the mountains of far-off Thessaly, and started an avalanche. She sank down beside him among the flowers that grew at his feet and hugged his legs, and spoke to him. As she spoke she raised her long arm and stroked his beard and touched his face.

"Father Zeus," she said, "I, Thetis, daughter of the Sea, present warmest greetings to mighty Zeus, King of the Gods, ruler of sky, air, and mountain. If I mention my name, oh heavenly one, it is because I fear you might have forgotten me. It has been many long painful hours since we last met."

"I have not forgotten you," said Zeus in a thunderous whisper. It was this unfortunate inability of his to whisper softly that upset so many of his nocturnes by catching Hera's sharp ears — even when he was conducting his session in some secret place upon some remote marg of beach or shelf of cliff.

"Thanks be for that," said Thetis. "For I think of you constantly."

"Constantly, my dear? But I understand you have many distractions."

"Oh, yes. I am a goddess, and grief does not become me. But even among the most sportive of my diversions my dreams shuttle your image like a girl weaving who, no matter what gray or blue threads embroider the detail of her design, still casts the strong scarlet flax which becomes the themeline of her tapestry. Thus does memory of you, my king, run its scarlet thread through the shuttling and weaving of my dreams."

"Sweet words, Thetis, which your voice makes even sweeter. What favor do you seek?"

"All-knowing Zeus, you have read my heart. Pleasure and longing alone would bring me to you. But now, as it happens, I do have a petition. Not for myself, but for my son, Achilles, the son of Peleus, my mortal husband, whom you will remember no doubt. And you will remember too that Achilles' days are briefly numbered. It has been decreed by the Fates that he could choose between brilliant fighting and death at Troy or a long life of peace and obscurity far from battle-cry and clash of spear. He chose Troy and death, of course. But since his days are to be so brief I do not wish them clouded by suffering. And Agamemnon makes him suffer brutal injustice."

"I do not understand," said Zeus. "Why does he not kill Agamemnon? Your son is no man to allow himself to be insulted."

"Aye, his sword had leaped halfway from its scabbard when your daughter, Athena, intervened, bidding him swallow his wrath and allow Agamemnon to work his horrid will. He has obeyed her, because she is your daughter and her strength derives from yours, as does that of all the gods. But he wishes to pay out Agamemnon all the same."

"What can I do at this juncture?" said Zeus.

"Inspire the Trojans to attack. Fire their hearts and strengthen their arms so that they are triumphant — so that Agamemnon must beg my son's pardon, or face defeat. For as you know Achilles is the very buckler of the Greek forces; without him, they must surely lose."

The frown on Zeus's face was darkening. Sable night itself seemed to flow from his beard and hair. Darkness thickened upon earth. Men groaned in their sleep, and the birds stopped singing.

"If I grant your favor, O Thetis, it means endless trouble for me. Night and day will Queen Hera rail and nag, haunt my pleasures and devil my repose. For she heavily favors the Greeks. And, knowing that I disagree, she has made me promise neutrality at least. But always she accuses me of secret partiality for the Trojans . . . which is true, of course. Now, if I do this thing for you, her opinion stands confirmed, and she will reveal her aptitude as arch-crone of the Universe."

"Please," said Thetis.

"I cannot refuse you," said Zeus. "But now return to the sea quickly lest she spot us talking here, and her suspicions be prematurely aroused. One kiss, my salty minx, and then off you go."

"Here's a kiss with all my heart. . . . And you do promise?"

"I do," said Zeus. "We shall have another conversation, perhaps, after the Greeks lose their battle."

"Gladly. . . . Do not keep me waiting too long, dear Zeus."

Thetis left Olympus, and sank to the depths of the sea. Zeus went into the banqueting hall of his Bronze Palace where the gods were gathered. But Hera was not disposed to let him eat the evening meal in peace.

"King of Deceivers!" she cried. "You have been with Thetis. And she has been asking you for favors. To help the Trojans, no doubt, because her bumptious brawling son has cooked up a grievance against the great Agamemnon."

"Good sister and wife," said Zeus. "Hera of the Golden

Throne — please shut your nagging mouth, and keep it shut, before I plant my fist in it."

"Abuse me! Beat me! You have the power, and can do it. But you have not the power to make me stop telling you what you should hear. I know that deep-sea witch has been flattering you, getting you to promise this and that. She's capable of anything, that one. Do you know how she spends her time? She hides behind reefs to capsize ships, so that she can swim off with her arms full of sailors — whom she keeps in a deep grotto. Then when they're old and feeble she feeds them to the sharks, and makes necklaces out of their fingerbones. She probably tells you that she spends her time doing kind deeds, and pining away for one more glimpse of your august visage. And you, you with all your tremendous wisdom, your insight into men's souls, you swallow this flattery like a green schoolboy, and promise her to do mischief to my Greeks."

Zeus said no word, but frowned so heavily that the stone floor began to crack. His fingers tightened around his scepter, a radiant volt-blue zigzag shaft of lighting. For he was also known as the Thunderer, Lord of Lightning — and, when angered, he would fling that deadly bolt the way a warrior hurls his lance.

Hephaestus, the smith-god, lame son of Zeus and Hera, who in his volcanic smithy had forged these lightning bolts and knew their awful power, ran to his mother in fear, whispering:

"Mother, mother, say something pleasant. Smile! Stop nagging! Or you'll get us all killed."

"Never," hissed Hera. "Let him flail about with his lightning bolt, let the brute do what he wishes. I shall never stop railing and howling until he disowns Thetis and her plots."

"Nay, mother, you forget. He has reason to favor Thetis of the Silver Feet, whatever her habits. Do not forget her ancient loyalty to him. When you and Athena and Poseidon plotted against him and tried to depose him from his throne — taking him by surprise, and binding him with a hundred knots — was it not she who called the hundred-handed Briareus, his titanic

37

gardener? Briareus rescued his master, each of his hundred hands untying a knot. Do you not remember? It was upon that terrible night too that he showed what his wrath could be — punishing us all, particularly you, chaining you upside down in the vault of heaven until your screams cracked the crystal goblets of the stars."

"I remember," muttered Hera hoarsely. "I remember."

"Then appease him, mother. Say something gentle, quickly. For his wrath is brewing. I see it plain. And terrible will be the consequences."

Hera arose then, and said: "Mighty Zeus, Lord of us all, I beg your pardon for causing you disquiet. It is only my concern for your peace of mind that sometimes leads me to hasty words. For I know how strong your honor is, how you value your word, and how you would hate to do anything to breach the promise of neutrality that you have given to me and Athena. So forgive my undue zeal in fearing that the tricks of Thetis would seduce you from your vow. Forgive me now, dear Lord, and I say not another word no matter what your intentions in the war below."

"Seat yourselves, all," boomed Zeus. "Drink your mead. We shall quarrel no more upon this night — for it is the shortest of all the year, and filled with the perfumes of earth." . . .

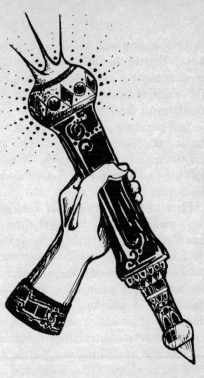

THE WAR COUNCIL

Zeus sent a Misleading Dream to Agamemnon. The dream masqueraded as Nestor who came to the king's tent at dawn, and said:

"Awake! Awake! This is no time to be sleeping. Hera has persuaded Zeus to permit the fall of Troy. So you must move immediately to the attack. Awake! Rouse yourself from slumber, and advance upon Troy. For gods grow wroth when men waste their favor."

Agamemnon arose immediately and called together his council. He related his dream. Nestor climbed to his feet, blushing with pride; it pleased him to appear in a dream sent by Zeus.

"It is a true auspice, O King, and must be obeyed. You know me well enough to realize I would never allow myself to appear in any dream that was not of the utmost authenticity."

39

Agamemnon said: "Nine years we have fought. We have killed Trojans, but Troy still stands. We have looted her colonies, sacked the cities of her allies, but Troy herself still abides, fair and impregnable as the virgin goddess, Artemis — who, indeed, favors the Trojan cause.

"After nine years our men are disheartened. Many of our finest have fallen to deadly Hector and his brothers, many others to Apollo's plague arrows. Now, I fear, too many of those left are on the point of mutiny or desertion. I have led men a long time; I know the signs.

"It is at this juncture that Zeus sees fit to promise me Troy. This means — and I interpret these matters not like an oracle but like a soldier — that he gives it to me if I can take it."

"Exactly," said Ulysses. "Therefore, let us take it."

"Yes, brave Ulysses. But consider this: If our men desert us in the midst of a general assault when we have committed our reserves to a headlong attack — then, indeed, we shall meet disaster."

"We must see that they do not desert," said Diomedes.

"Precisely what I propose," said Agamemnon. "What I mean to do is weed out the cowards and traitors beforehand. I shall call the men together, and address them in discouraging terms, indicating that I am ready to abandon the war and sail back to Greece."

"Dangerous, very dangerous," said Ulysses. "They will welcome your words and stampede to the boats."

"And that will weed out the cowards and traitors."

"You may be weeding out the entire army — saving those present, of course. Your test is ill-timed, O Agamemnon. The men are war-weary, and legitimately so. The plague proves that. Despite the venom of Apollo's arrows, a man in good spirits is bucklered against disease. But a sick body means a sick soul. And they are battle-worn; they long for home. Your speech will send them scurrying off to the ships."

"Then what would you have me do?" cried Agamemnon. "If

things are that bad we may as well fold our tents, raise our sails, and skulk away for home."

"No," said Ulysses. "The important thing is to ignore the men's weariness, and show them a glad and confident face. Address the troops. Speak no discouraging word, but tell them your dream and order them to attack. Twenty years of warfare have taught me that the cure for fear is fighting."

"Too many words," growled huge Ajax. "Let's stop talking and start cracking some heads. If we crack enough outside of Troy we'll soon be doing it inside."

But Agamemnon would not be dissuaded. Like all men of few ideas he clung bitterly to one when it occurred. And by now he had convinced himself that his notion was a brilliant one.

"I shall make the speech I planned," he said. "And depend upon you, kings and chieftains of my War Council, to keep the men from breaking."

Agamemnon issued orders. Nine heralds went throughout the camp blowing their silver trumpets, calling the men together. They came in a mighty swarm. Even after its losses this army remained the greatest fighting force ever assembled in ancient times.

Agamemnon stood on a rock and raised his golden scepter. He had planned his speech for hours, but was able to utter only one sentence.

"Friends — my heart has been overwhelmed by our losses, and I have decided it is time to quit this war and sail for Greece."

No sooner had he said these words, than, as Ulysses had foretold, the vast crowd stampeded. With a wild moaning cry the men leaped to their feet and stormed toward the beach. Had the restless gods not been vigilant the Greek cause would have died that day.

But Hera and Athena were watching from Olympus.

"What's the matter with Agamemnon," cried Hera. "Has he gone quite mad? Oh, this is some treachery of Zeus, I'm quite certain."

"No, this is Agamemnon's own stupidity," said Athena. "Some idea of testing the men before battle. And he shouldn't be having ideas, he's not equipped."

"They're stampeding like cattle," said Hera. "Look at the miserable cowards. And when I think of the effort we've spent on them. Go, dear stepdaughter. Descend to Troy, and stop them."

"Divine stepmother, I go," said Athena — and she flew down to Troy.

She did not reveal herself to the multitude, only to her favorite, Ulysses, saying to him: "Don't just stand there, man. Stop them."

She snapped her fingers. Agamemnon's heavy scepter flew from his hand and sailed over the heads of the mob. She caught it in midair and handed it to Ulysses.

"Here is the rod of power. The very staff and scepter of kingly authority, given only by the gods — and to be taken back at will. Grasp the scepter, Ulysses. Use it. Stop the rabble's flight."

With great strides Ulysses leaped down to the beach, bearing his scepter. Divinely inspired, his shout of outrage rolled like thunder across the plain.

"Stop!" he roared. "Stop! I command it! And I speak the will of the gods."

He rushed up and down the strand, guarding the beached ships so that no one could board them. His flailing scepter rose like a golden barrier before the men's astonished eyes. In truth, with his red hair blazing, and his eyes flashing, and the golden rod flailing, he looked like a god descended.

"Stop!" he shouted. "Back to the assembly-place. Agamemnon means battle, not retreat. You misunderstood his words; they were only a rhetorical device. You fools, you dimwitted dolts. Zeus himself has appeared to the king in his sleep, ordering an attack upon Troy. Do you think this is the moment he would order us to sail home? You have misunderstood. You have listened with your fears instead of your intelligence. No wonder you heard things wrong. Back! Back! Back to the arena. Let the king declare your battle array."

Listening to Ulysses, seeing him blaze with that special creative rage which comes rarely in a lifetime, and then only to extraordinary men because it is a particle of the gods' own radiance, hearing Ulysses' clangorous voice, and seeing him guard the ships, the men felt courage slipping back into their hearts, and began to drift away from the beach.

But a gifted troublemaker arose. Thersites was his name, a little hunched shuffling bald-headed man, very clever, with a voice that brayed like a donkey's so that you could hear no one whom he wished to drown out. Now he said:

"You stupid sheep, do you allow yourself to be herded this way by a man with a staff? For the first time in his life that lout, Agamemnon, speaks the truth. By accident, I know, but the truth all the same. This war *is* a disaster, and the sooner we get home the better. It's a bloody miracle there are any of us left to get home after nine years of so-called leadership by greedy, inept, cowardly imitations of kings. So heed not this red-headed madman, my fellow-soldiers, but board the ships. And if any of these brave chieftains come after you and try to drag you back, why then, cut their throats and dump them overboard as a sacrifice to Poseidon, who will ensure us cloudless skies and a following wind."

It was part of Ulysses' wisdom always to listen to criticism, hoping to learn something thereby. So he held his hand until Thersites finished his speech. Then, by way of comment, he swung his scepter. The knobbed end hit Thersites in the face, shattering his jaw. Thersites tried to keep talking but the only sound that came out was the crackling of broken bone. He kept trying to speak, then gagged on his own blood, and fell unconscious to the ground.

By this time the other members of the War Council — Ajax

the Greater, Ajax the Lesser, Idmoneus, Nestor, Diomedes — had joined Ulysses, and stood between the men and the ships, thrusting the men back, exhorting them. The mutiny crumbled. The men turned and moved sullenly back to the field. Ulysses and the other chieftains followed, herding them. When they were again assembled he mounted Agamemnon's rock, still holding the golden scepter. Agamemnon himself, seized by bewilderment and rage, had vanished into his tent. Ulysses said:

"Our great king and war-leader, Agamemnon, has been so disgusted by your cowardly performance that he does not wish to address you again today, and has asked me to say a few words. Let me say, men, that, despite appearances, I do not view your recent abrupt withdrawal toward the beach as cowardice. I view it as a gigantic form of the fighting man's gesture whereby, before he can strike his blow, must draw back his arm. You were not running away; you were coiling for the spring, the spring that will take you in one tigerish leap over the walls and into Troy. I promise you this, men, and I do not speak idly: We will have victory. For know that on the night that has just passed, father Zeus himself condescended to visit Agamemnon in a dream, promising us victory if we attack, attack, attack."

On the third repetition of the word "attack" he flung up his arm, the scepter flashed, and the men raised a great ferocious joyful shout. Two brown vultures coasting the steeps of air off Mt. Ida, heard this yelling, and planed down a way. For they had heard this sound before and knew that it meant a battle, and a battle meant fine feasting afterward.

THE BATTLE BEGINS

The Greek forces advanced toward Troy, raising an enormous cloud of dust. And the dust was the color of gold mixed with the color of blood. For, at Ulysses' suggestion, they were advancing on the western wall of Troy that afternoon so that the Trojans would have to fight with the setting sun in their eyes. This was one of the oldest tricks in warfare, but still effective, and Ulysses never overlooked the slightest advantage.

The great bronze gates of the western wall swung open, and the men of Troy came out to meet the attackers. The high gods settled down comfortably on the peaks of Olympus to watch the sport.

Through the dust-cloud Teucer, who had the sharpest eyes among the Greeks, spotted something strange. He reported to Agamemnon, who held up his hand in the sign of halt. The dust subsided, and the attackers saw an amazing spectacle. The Trojan line had stopped moving and was standing fast, weapons glittering in the slanted rays of the sun. And a single man was coming forward to meet them — a tall, supple figure clad in a panther skin and carrying two spears. It was Paris, who raised his voice in challenge:

"Hear me, O Greeks. I propose single combat between the lines to any one of you bold enough to come forward and meet me."

"Rumor travels fast," grumbled Ulysses to himself. "It's clear they've already heard about Achilles' defection. Otherwise that coxcomb would never be offering single combat."

Menelaus then split the air with his war-cry, and shuffled forward. His shout was echoed by all the Greeks, for it was very fitting that he, the offended husband, should respond to the challenge of the abductor.

"I'll fight you!" he cried. "And a short fight it will be. I'll tear out your guts with my bare hands."

Now Menelaus was no comfortable sight for an opponent. If his brother, Agamemnon, was a bull, he was a bear. Not very tall, but very wide, and bulging with muscle, clothed in a pelt of black hair from neck to ankle. Black-bearded, wearing black armor — helmet, breastplate, and greaves not of bronze like most of the others, but of iron — too heavy for most men to wear; iron pieces smoky and black as if they had just issued from Hephaestus' forge. He carried an axe in one hand, and a huge iron-bossed bullhide shield in the other. Truly he was a fearsome sight slouching out of the Greek lines like an iron bear.

Paris took one look and darted back into the Trojan lines, crying: "It's not fair! He has full armor. I am clad only in a panther skin. I'll fight any man alive, but a metal monster is something else!"

His brother Hector, commander of the Trojan forces, turned on him.

"You miserable cringing coward, you yellow-bellied dog. The

oracle was right. You *will* bring disgrace and ruin on us all. Here we are, fighting a war started by you, and when a chance is given for you to strike a blow for yourself — something you should have been praying to the gods for — you skulk away. My father was right in his original impulse. He should have garroted you with your own umbilical cord. Dreadful was my mother's misjudgment, saving you. Well, you are not free to disgrace yourself. You are a son of Priam, and when you bring shame on yourself, you shame us all. I will not permit this. Sooner will I break your pretty skull, here and now, explain that you have met with an unfortunate accident, and take up your challenge to Menelaus myself."

Paris, who thought quickly, said: "Peace, brother. It was I who issued the challenge — unprompted by you — and it is I who will fight. Please do not scourge me with that tongue of yours. You are my elder brother — my leader — but you have no right to say such things to me, because I chose to lighten the heavy moment with a jest or two. Truly, the thing I regret most about this war I started is that every day it makes the Trojans more like the Greeks. We are forgetting what laughter is. And that is a terrible casualty."

"I do not follow you," said Hector. "Speak plainly. Are you going to fight or not?"

"Certainly, I'm going to fight. I didn't come to battle to exchange platitudes with you. But that man is clad in ugly armor from woolly pate to tufted toe. I, too, must armor myself."

"Brothers, lend him some pieces of armor," said Hector. "I'll start. Take my shield."

"Nay, brother," said Paris. "It is too heavy for me. Troilus here will give me what I need. We are the same size."

And from Troilus, the brother next youngest to himself, also a very beautiful lad, he borrowed helmet, chestplate, and greaves. From Lyncaeus, an elder brother, he took a bronze-bossed oxhide shield.

While Paris was armoring himself, Hector stepped out between the two armies and held up his arms for silence.

"Worthy foes," he said. "You have known me for nine long years and know that I do not shrink from a fight. So you will not take my proposal in the wrong spirit. But I think there is a kind of inspired justice about the idea of Paris and Menelaus meeting each other in single combat. Now I suggest this: If Paris wins, we keep Helen, and you depart, taking with you only the price of Helen's bride-gift, which we will repay to Menelaus, or to his brother if Menelaus does not survive the fight. If, on the other hand, Menelaus leaves Paris in the dust, then he must take back his wife, plus an indemnity to be reckoned by joint council between us. Then, your cause having been won, you depart on your black ships in honor and in peace."

There was a great clamor of joyful shouting on both sides. It was clear that Hector's proposal met with general favor from Trojan and Greek alike. Ulysses saw Agamemnon frown, and knew that the hasty general was about to refuse Hector's offer, and order a charge. Ulysses went swiftly to Agamemnon, and whispered: "Agree . . . agree. . . . We'll have general mutiny if you refuse. And the end will be the same. The oracle has decreed that Troy must fall, and fall she must, for the voice of the oracle is the promise of the gods. But for now, agree to the truce. There is nothing else to do."

Therefore, Agamemnon answered, saying: "Well spoken, Hector. Let our brothers fight."

Hector stepped out between the armies, holding his helmet in his hand. In the helmet were two pebbles, a rough one for Menelaus, a smooth one for Paris. He shook his helmet; one pebble jumped out — the smooth one. A groan went up from the Greek lines because this meant that Paris would cast the first spear. The Trojans cheered wildly.

Paris danced out into the space between the armies. Menelaus shuffled forward to meet him, covering himself with his bullhide shield. Paris came, all glittering bronze, poising two bronze-headed spears. He stopped about twenty paces from his enemy and hurled his spear. Its point hit the iron boss of Menelaus' shield and fell to earth. Now the Trojans groaned and the Greeks cheered. Menelaus immediately hurled his spear with tremendous force. It hummed venomously through the air, and sheared through the Trojan's shield. Paris ducked aside and the spearhead only nicked his shoulder. Before he could recover, Menelaus was upon him hacking away with his axe. Paris tried to back away but Menelaus allowed him no time to recover. Menelaus raised his axe high and smote the Trojan's horse-plume helmet. Paris staggered but the axe-head shattered into three pieces.

"Cruel Zeus!" cried Menelaus. "First you raise my hopes by allowing me to close with the falsehearted homebreaker. Then when he is in my grasp you save him from my spear; you break my axe — leave me weaponless. But I have weapons still — these two good hands you gave me before you gave me sword and spear — and they are enough to do the beautiful murder I have dreamed of for nine long years."

He grasped Paris by the crest of his helmet, swung him off his feet, and began to drag him back toward the Greek lines. Paris struggled helplessly; his legs were dragging, the chinstrap of his helmet dug into his throat, strangling him.

But Aphrodite could not bear to see her favorite being manhandled. Making herself invisible she flew down from Olympus, broke the chinstrap of his helmet and snatched him away, leaving the raging Menelaus with an empty helmet in his hands.

Paris felt himself translated into paradise. Instead of strangling beneath his enemy's hands he was lying snug as a babe in Aphrodite's arms, cuddled against her breast. The goddess kept herself invisible as the wind but he recognized her by her intoxicating scent — which was honey and baking bread. Aphrodite flew over the Trojan wall, past the painted wooden houses and the marble temple, to Priam's castle. She flew through a casement and deposited Paris in his own bed. Then, still invisible, she kissed him into a healing sleep.

Down on the battlefield the disappearance of Paris had ignited angry confusion. Trojan and Greek began a shifting and muttering but no one was quite sure what had happened. Agamemnon then stepped between the lines, raising his arms for silence.

Honorable Hector, Trojans, all — I declare my brother Menelaus, King of Sparta, the victor in the single combat we agreed was to decide the war. To this you must submit since your champion Paris has vanished and Menelaus holds the field. Therefore, Helen must be returned to us, and the entire cost of our expedition must be paid by you, plus a huge and fitting indemnity."

The Greeks shouted with joy. The Trojan lines were wrapped in bitter silence.

Helen had been watching on the wall, with Priam and the other elders of Troy. When she heard Agamemnon's declaration she hurried back to the palace to change her dress, perfume herself, and prepare to be retaken. She was amazed to find Paris in her room.

"What are you doing here?"

"Sleeping . . . waiting. . . ."

"For what?"

"For you, dear. What else?"

"I was watching from the wall. The last I saw of you, you were fighting Menelaus, more or less. Did you run away, darling?"

"More or less. Not exactly."

"You didn't exactly stay either."

"Rough character, that exhusband of yours. No one stays around him very long. . . ."

"What now, sweet coward?"

"Come here."

"But I'm about to be reclaimed. Agamemnon has declared the Greeks victorious."

"Agamemnon is hasty, my dear. The gods are just beginning to enjoy this war. They're not going to let it end so quickly."

"Are you sure?"

50

"Believe me, the real war is just beginning. And we battle-weary warriors need frequent interludes of tender repose. So come here."

Hera and Athena were now perched on the same peak whispering to each other; they did not like the way things were going down below. Zeus called out teasingly:

"Well, my dears, your gentle impulses should be gratified, for it looks very much like peace will be concluded between Greece and Troy, and many brave men spared who would otherwise have died."

"You are hasty, sire," said Hera sweetly. "No peace treaty has been signed, only an armistice. And with two armies full of such spirited warriors, anything may happen to break a truce. Of course, we hope nothing does, but — after all — it has been foretold that Troy will fall."

Zeus frowned, and did not answer. He knew better than to try to match gibes with Hera. In the meantime the ox-eyed queen of the gods was whispering to Athena:

"We must do something immediately, or peace will break out. Get down there and see what you can do about ending this stupid truce."

Athena flew down and whispered to a Trojan leader named Pandarus. "The man who sends an arrow through one of those famed Greek warriors will live in the annals of warfare for the next three thousand years — longer perhaps. Just imagine putting a shaft through Ulysses, or Agamemnon, or Achilles. No, he's not fighting today, is he? Or Menelaus. Look, there Menelaus stands, still searching for Paris. He's within very easy bowshot. What are you waiting for, man? If I were an archer like you I wouldn't hesitate for a second."

Pandarus swallowed this flattery in one gulp, as Athena knew he would. Now, Pandarus was a fine archer, although not as good as he thought he was, and he owned a marvellous bow made of two polished antelope horns seized together by copper bands, and strung with ox sinew. Inflamed by Athena's words, he snatched an arrow from his quiver, fitted it to his bow-string, bent his horn-bow, and let fly. The arrow sang through the air and would have finished off Menelaus right then and there had not Athena, making herself invisible, flashed across the space and deflected the arrow so that it struck through the Spartan king's buckle and, still further deflected, passed through the bottom part of his breastplate, just scratching his side. The wound looked more serious than it was because the arrow stuck out the other side of his breastplate as if it had passed through his body. Menelaus staggered and fell to his knees; blood flowed down his thighs. The Greek army gasped with horror, and the Trojans groaned too, for they knew this must break the truce. Agamemnon uttered a mighty grief-stricken shout:

"Traitors! You have killed my brother! You have broken the truce! Greeks — to arms! Kill the traitors! Charge!"

The dust was churned again as the whole Greek army, moving as one man, snatched up its weapons and rushed toward the Trojan lines.

All this time, while the battle was raging back and forth, Achilles kept to his tent and did not come out. He lay on his pallet trying to shut his ears to the sound of battle. But he could not. He heard it all — war-cry and answer, challenge and reply. Spear-shock and the crash of shields; the rattle of sword against helmet, the ping of dart against breast-plate. Arrows sang through the air. Men shrieked and groaned; horses neighed and bugled. This sound had always been music to him — the best sound in all the world — but now it was a simple torment. For there to be a battle going on and Achilles not in it was a thing absolutely against nature. Great sobs wrenched Achilles. But Patroclus was in the tent too, waiting with him, and he did not wish his friend to hear his grief.

So Achilles bit down on his wrist till it bled, stifling his sobs that way. At last he could bear it no longer, but arose from his bed and washed his face in the cold water that stood in a golden ewer, one he had taken in some half-forgotten raid. Oh, happy days they seemed now, before his quarrel with Agamemnon, when he could allow himself to roam the seas raiding the home-islands of Trojan allies, raging into their very fastnesses, spearing men like fish, and sacking the proud castles of their treasures — and taking many slaves.

He stood now at the portal of his tent watching the battle. He saw Diomedes sweeping up and down, and it was like some memory of himself. He groaned aloud. Patroclus came to him and put his arm around his neck.

"Old friend," said Patroclus, "beloved comrade — I cannot see you kill yourself with grief. Forget your feud with Agamemnon. Go fight! Arm yourself and join the battle. Else regret will tear your breast more surely than enemy spear."

"I cannot bury my feud with Agamemnon," cried Achilles. "False friend! How can you tell me to do that? He insulted me, took Briseis. Do you think I will allow any man, though he be king a dozen times, to do such things to me? No! I would rather fight with the Trojans against the Greeks."

"A traitor to your own kind? No, you would never be that," said Patroclus.

"I'm a traitor to my own nature if I do not fight. And that's worse."

"You could never bring yourself to fight your old companions. How could you level your spear against either of the Ajaxes, or Ulysses, or Idomeneus? I do not even mention myself."

Achilles took his friend's head between his hands and looked deep into his eyes.

"Oh, Patroclus," he said. "You would be surprised to know the names of those I could bring myself to fight when the battle-fury burns. I like them well — Ajax, and Diomedes, Ulysses, Idomeneus, even that crude bear, Menelaus. I have adventured with them, and raided with them, and fought the Trojans with them. I should regret killing them, perhaps, but I could manage the deed in the heat of battle. Only you, my friend, have a true hold on my esteem. You I will never harm. You I will always avenge should anyone else offer you harm. I feel myself being torn in two. I feel a fire inside my head that is scorching my very capacity to think. I feel a pain in my gut that is worse than any weapon that has pierced my armor. I don't know what will happen to me in the days to come, but take this pledge: You are my friend, my true friend, sweet cousin and companion of my boyhood; I shall never harm you, and shall take vengeance upon anyone who does."

He shoved Patroclus away. "Go now. I know you do not wish me to stand alone, but I pray you, go. For I do not wish you to see my grief.

"I go," said Patroclus. "But I shall not join the battle either until you give me leave."

He walked off, but not far. He circled in back of the tent and stood there watching Achilles. For his heart was sodden with love for the mighty youth, and he was as loyal as a dog.

Hera and Athena watched, frowning, from their peak on Olympus as the Trojans beat back the Greeks.

"What ails you, stepdaughter?" said Hera. "You seem to be losing your touch. The strength you gave Diomedes appears to have ebbed, and with it the tide of Greek fortunes. Look at them; they're running like rabbits."

"It is because my brothers have broken their vow of neutrality," said Athena angrily. "Apollo has completely restored Aeneas who was felled by Diomedes in a glorious action, and the son of Anchises wields his weapon more powerfully than ever before. And Hector has suddenly become inspired, and is raging like a wolf on the field. But it is no accident. Behind him I see the form of Ares goading the Trojans to superhuman effort."

"Yes, Ares is chiefly to blame," said Hera. "Although I am his mother, I must confess he is an incorrigible mischiefmaker. Apollo will mend wounds and issue edicts, but he is too proud to fight with mortals. Ares, however, exults in battle, no matter whom he is fighting. And it is he who harries the Trojans for-

54

ward. Yes, it is Ares who must be driven from the field. And it is you who must do it, stepdaughter. For Zeus would never forgive me if I took up arms against my own son. He is quite hidebound in some respects."

"Very well," said Athena. "Then I shall do it. For many a century now I have been wanting to settle scores with that lout."

So saying, she sped to earth and, keeping herself invisible, joined the Greeks where they had set up a defense line near their ships. The Trojans were driving ahead viciously, but the toughest Greek warriors — Ajax the Greater, Ajax the Lesser, Teucer, Ulysses, Idomeneus, Agamemnon, Menelaus — all these ferocious fighters formed knots of resistance to the Trojans, who had breached the Greek line in many places, and were advancing upon the beached ships.

Athena spoke to Diomedes, appearing before him in her own guise, but keeping herself invisible to the others.

"Son of Tydeus," she said. "You are a great sorrow and disappointment to me. After a few hours of fighting you grow weary. You fail. You leave the field to Hector and Aeneas. It's incredible. Standing there on Olympus I could scarcely believe what I was seeing. I did not know how to answer to mother Hera who chided, and justly, for choosing so weak a vessel to hold the beautiful rage of the gods. I am grieved, Diomedes. I am shocked and dismayed."

By this time Diomedes' face was wet with tears. He tore out his beard in great handfuls.

"Another word of reproof, O Athena," he shouted, "and I shall plunge this blade into my breast. And you shall have to find another to crush with your scorn. Why do you blame me for that which is not my fault. You saw me overcoming every Trojan I met, even Pandarus, the shrewd archer, even the mighty Aeneas. Why, I even wounded his mother, Aphrodite! And how many men have dappled with ichor the radiant flesh of the goddess of love? But in the midst of these deeds I was stopped by your brother, Apollo, the sun-god himself, who

55

warned me that I must never lift my hand against an Olympian again, threatening me with eternal torment if I disobeyed. So what am I to do? For it is your other brother, Ares, who ranges behind the Trojan lines, filling Aeneas and Hector with battle-rage, and making them invincible. Unless I lift my spear against Ares and chase him from the field he will never allow me to measure my strength with Hector and Aeneas."

"You speak truly," said Athena. "But Apollo cannot stop *me* from fighting Ares. I have the permission of mother Hera. As for Zeus, he detests his brawling son. Many a time, in aeons gone, he was moved to punish Ares himself. And although father Zeus tends to favor the Trojans I know he will not chide me overmuch if I chastise Ares. Let us go then. You will lift your spear against him, but I will ride as your charioteer and guide your spear. And I will be your buckler too when the god of war aims his gigantic lance at your breastplate. Come, brave Diomedes, we will teach the Trojans that the Greeks must prevail even though great Achilles disdains to take the field. Yes, I will be your charioteer, and guide these marvellous horses you have taken from Aeneas, and you shall be able to devote your full time to fighting."

So saying, Athena sprang into the chariot and took up the reins. Diomedes stood beside her couching his spear and shouting his war cry. Athena drove directly toward Ares, where he was snorting like a wild boar over a pile of dead Greeks, and despoiling them of their armor. He wished to take back to Olympus the gear of twenty men of large stature to give to Hephaestus, who would then melt the metal down and forge a breastplate and pair of greaves large enough for Ares. But when he saw the chariot approach, the somber pits of his eyes glowed with a new greed; he wanted those horses for himself. Also he wished very much to square accounts with Diomedes, who had been so terrible against the Trojans that day. He picked up his twenty-foot spear, the shaft of which was an entire ash tree, and rushed toward the chariot. It was a charge such as could batter down a city gate, but Athena reached out her mailed hand and deflected the spearhead so that it whizzed harmlessly past Diomedes, carrying Ares within easy sword-reach. Diomedes' quick counterstroke half-gutted Ares. He fell with a horrid screech clutching his stomach. Had he been a mortal man the wound would have been fatal. As it was, he had to quit the field and fly back to Olympus. He visited Hephaestus first, who tucked his mighty guts in place, and sewed up the wound with bullhide sinew.

Then Ares stormed into Zeus' throne-room, crying: "Justice! Justice! That harpy daughter of yours, that owl-hag Athena rides invisible as Diomedes' charioteer, guarding him from all harm, and strengthening his hands so that he kills, kills, kills."

"Fancy that," said Zeus. "I had no idea that killing was so distasteful to you. These scruples seem to have developed overnight."

"You do not understand, O Zeus. It is not only mortals he attacks. Earlier today he wounded Aphrodite. Just now he bloodied me with a lucky thrust. Me! Your son! God of Battle!"

"Who are you to complain?" shouted Zeus. "She should not be taking a direct hand in the fighting, it is true, for I have forbidden it. But you were doing the very same thing on the Trojan side. I saw you. You were disguised as Acamas, and with your own weapons were killing Greeks and despoiling them of their armor. You are equally to blame, and if I punish one I shall punish both. Besides . . . I think the God of war should be ashamed to publicize his defeat at the hands of his sister."

"Sister? That's no sister," muttered Ares as he left the throne-room. "That's a harpy out of hell."

Nevertheless, Zeus sent Apollo after Ares to make sure that his wound had been properly tended, and also sent lightfooted Iris to recall Athena from the battlefield. He then issued another edict against direct intervention by any god on one side or the other.

HECTOR

                The battle had begun at dawn, and it was now the hot middle of the day. The sun hung in the sky like a brass helmet; dust hung in the air hot as metal filings. The exhausted men gasped like unwatered cattle. They could feel their flesh charring where the sun hit their armor. Many of them threw off their armor and fought naked. Shaft of spear and lance, and hilt of sword, were so slippery with sweat that they slid out of men's hands. Without any orders being given the fighting subsided, and the armies drew off a little way from one another to await the cool of late afternoon.

    During this lull Hector returned to Troy. He had two errands: First, to dig his brother Paris out of the boudoir and get him onto the battlefield; secondly, to visit his wife, Andromache.

58

Andromache was not at home. The servants told him she was waiting on the Scaeian Wall. He went there to find her. They embraced. She said: "You're so hot and tired. Must you rush back to the battlefield? Can't you stay with me awhile? Stay, only a little while, and let me make you comfortable again."

"No, I must get back there, dearly as I should love to stay with you and pass some cool and delicious hours in your matchless company. But I am the commander, and must lead my men."

"You look so solemn — so sad. Have you come to tell me something special?"

"I have had a vision of Troy's defeat. And among all the scenes of carnage and disaster it drags in its wake, all I can see is one picture: You, in time to come, have been borne away by some mailed conqueror to faroff Greece. And there in Argos, or in Attica, or Sparta, I see you dressed in dull clothing, spinning at the loom, or drawing water under the eye of your mistress — who will not be partial to you for you will be too beautiful, more beautiful than she, whoever she be. And her husband, your master, will be spending his nights with you rather than with her. I see you a servant, a slave. That is what losing means — to be enslaved. And that sight of you there fills me with such sorrowful rage that I feel a giant's strength, feel that I, personally, could interpose my body between Troy and all the Greek hordes — even if my comrades are cut down — and kill and kill until there is not one Greek left. And so the vision brings its own contradiction. And what do you make of that?"

"What do I make of that? That you are very brave, and very dear. And that I am blessed beyond all women in my husband. For you, I believe, are the mightiest man ever to bear arms, and the noblest heart ever to bear another's grief. And when you meet Achilles, or Ajax, the gods will favor your cause, for you are living proof that their handiwork is excelling itself."

"Thank you for those words," said Hector. "They are the

sweetest I have ever heard in all my life. It is true, whether I can conquer Achilles or not, I must challenge him to single combat. These pitched battles waste our forces too much, and we do not have as many men to spare as do the enemy. Yes, I shall fight the strong Achilles, and when I do the memory of your loving words will make a victor's music in my ears."

He took his infant son from the nurse's arms. Lifting him high as if stretching him toward the heavens, he said: "Great Zeus, father of us all, hear a lesser father's prayer. I am a warrior; some call me a hero, and, as you know, a degree of self-esteem attaches to that condition. Instead of sacrificing a bull to you then, let me sacrifice my self-esteem — which, I assure you, is as huge and hotblooded and rampaging as any bull. Let me ask you this: That when my son is grown and fights his battles, as all men must, and returns therefrom, that men will say of him only this. 'He is a better man than his father was.' "

The baby was frightened by his father's nodding horsetail plume, and burst into tears. Hector smiled and kissed him, and gave him into his mother's arms. Then he kissed her, and said: "I must be off now, good wife. I must rout out lazy Paris and try to prevail upon him to do a bit of fighting in this war that he started. Farewell."

But it took him a while to press through the mob. It seemed all Troy was out in the streets. Since he was their special hero, the people crowded about him, shouting questions, trying to touch him. He kept a smile on his face, but forced his way steadily through the mob. However, his son's nurse had been so moved by his words on the wall that she had rushed off to tell everyone she could find what her master had said. By the time he reached Paris' house all Troy was buzzing with his speech to Andromache, and no woman who heard it could refrain from bursting into tears, and thinking critically of her own husband.

He found Paris with Helen, polishing his armor.

"It's clean enough, brother — too clean. I should prefer to see it bloodied a bit."

"Ah, the old complaint," murmured Paris.

60

"Yes, the old complaint. You do not fight enough in your behalf, Paris. You set a bad example to the troops, and create rancor among your brothers. The word has spread that you are a coward. I too have called you that in the heat of my displeasure, and yet I know that you are not. You are too proud for cowardice. What you are is irresponsible. You cannot bear the discipline of warfare. The compulsion, the iron urgency. You are like some magic child who can do anything, but views his own caprice as the basic law of the universe. Well, you must drop that. For the cruel necessity of war is upon us — a war prompted by your own desires. And you must play not only an honorable role, but a hero's role. Zeus knows we need all the heroes we can muster."

"You keep saying these things, Hector," said Paris. "But I haven't uttered one syllable of objection. Why do you think I'm polishing my armor. I never wear it to bed. A rumor, incidentally, that is whispered about you, big brother. No, I mean to go to battle; I just want to look nice when I'm there."

"Dear brother Hector," said Helen. "Honorable commander. I know you think little of me. I know you consider me a shameless woman who seduced your brother and plunged Troy into a dreadful war. Nevertheless, let me say this: I, too, am always after him to do his share of fighting. I am of warrior race too, you know. In fact, it is said that a very prominent belligerent, Zeus himself, is my father. I don't know how much truth there is in it, but they say he wooed my mother in the shape of a swan, and that I was born from a swan's egg — which accounts for my complexion."

She smiled at Hector, and he could find no word of reproach to say to her. In the blaze of Helen's smile no man could remain wrathful. Even iron Hector was not immune.

"And I heard what you said to Andromache," said Helen. A single pearly tear trembled on her eyelash without falling. "I think it was the most beautiful thing any man has ever said to any wife. This scoundrel here could never in a million years find such sentiments on his tongue, and he is famous for sweet

61

speech. Truly the thought of being enslaved is something that haunts every Trojan woman and devils every warrior."

"Truly," drawled Paris. "No man likes to think of his wife being enslaved by anyone but himself. Quite intolerable."

"See . . . he jokes even at that," cried Helen. "What is one to do with him?"

"Make a soldier of him," growled Hector. "Come on, prettyboy, enough talk — let's fight."

Paris knelt before Helen, took both her hands, turned them over, and kissed each palm. Then he closed her hands.

"Keep these until I come again."

The sight of Hector and Paris emerging from the gate, fresh and shining, brought new heart to the Trojans, and they charged the Greek positions again. Led by Hector, Paris, and Aeneas, they wrought great havoc among the enemy, who lost some of their best warriors in that flurry.

Athena, despite Zeus' edict, flew down from Olympus to help the Greeks. This time she was intercepted by Apollo, who said:

"No, sister, you must not. You are Zeus' favorite daughter, as everyone knows, and you should be the last to flout his commands. You see that I am keeping aloof from the battle, and so must you."

"I can't," cried Athena. "I won't! Too many Greeks are being killed."

"Come away. Listen to me. I have a plan to end this slaughter — without any direct intercession on our part."

Athena joined Apollo under a huge oak tree.

"Owl-goddess," he said. "We can stop this killing by arranging that the battle be settled through single combat. This was attempted earlier in the day when Paris challenged Menelaus, but Paris fled, and the idea came to nought. Now, however, we shall have great Hector issue the challenge, and you may be sure that he will fight to the finish."

"I agree," said Athena. "Let us send Hector the idea."

Gods send ideas to men in different ways. But whatever way they choose it is necessary to create the illusion of personal authorship — that is, that each man believe the idea to be his own. The gods' idea came to Hector as a dart of sunlight glancing off the tall helm of Ajax which towered above his companions. Seeing that high helmet gleam Hector said to Paris:

"Listen, brother, I have an idea."

Paris was willing enough to stop fighting and listen. Aeneas drew close too. So did the other sons of Priam. And the fighting was eased again as the Trojans held a council on the field.

"We have fought valiantly this day," said Hector. "And have prevented the Greeks from storming our walls, which was their intention this morning. So, in a sense, we have won the battle. In another sense we have not. Nor can we win any head-to-head battle with the Greeks. For if our losses be equal or anywhere near equal they will contribute toward our final defeat. The Greeks outnumber us, and we dare not match their losses, or even match half their losses, or by and by we shall find ourselves with no fighting men at all while they will have a force capable of taking the city. What I propose then is this: That I challenge one of their champions to single combat, and that the honors of the day rest upon the result. If I win I shall do this each day until either I shall have run through all their champions and so dishearten them that they must depart, or I myself am killed, leaving the decisions to someone else. Let me add that the absence of Achilles should be no little help to this project."

His words met with general favor. He stepped in front of the Trojan lines, and addressed the Greeks.

"Honorable foemen," he said, "you have fought long and well upon this day, and have killed many of us. We have fought no less honorably and have killed many of you. But the sun sinks now and we have supplied the vultures with food enough for this day. Let me be a surrogate for the Trojan deaths, and choose you a champion who will meet me and be a surrogate for your deaths. Upon our combat let rest the honors of the day. If I lose, the victor may strip me of my armor, nor will any of my brothers oppose him. All I ask is that my body be returned to my father, Priam, for decent burning. But if the gods favor me in this combat, then I will act in the same way toward my fallen foe. Come, then — let me hear! Who of you will fight me? I await your reply."

His voice blared like a trumpet across the lines, leaving silence after it. The Greek champions looked at each other. No one, it seemed, was rushing to volunteer. Finally, Menelaus dragged himself to his feet, and said:

"Well, I won one duel today. Maybe this is my day for winning. If none of you offers to fight him, then I must."

But Agamemnon pulled him back.

"No, brother, not you. In plain words, if you fight Hector, you will die. The man belongs with the greatest warriors of all time. Everyone acknowledges this. Even our own Achilles, for all his murderous pride, has never seen fit to engage Hector in single combat."

"Someone must fight him!" cried Menelaus. "If not I, then someone else."

"For shame!" cried old Nestor, rising and berating them in his dry voice like an angry cricket. "For shame. . . . How the generations have shrunk! There were mighty men in my day. How they would laugh and scoff to see you sitting here like a circle of schoolboys awaiting the master's rod! Come . . . if there is no one to volunteer then we must draw lots and let the gods choose."

He took chips of wood and inscribed the names of the Greek champions — nine of them — the two Ajaxes, Teucer, Idomeneus, Diomedes, Ulysses, Agamemnon, Menelaus, and Nestor's own son, Antilochus, a very skillful charioteer. He shook the chips in his helmet, then selected one, read the name inscribed in a piercing voice.

"Ajax," he said. "Ajax of Salamis. Known as the Great Ajax."

To Hector, Ajax looked as big as Ares prowling out of the

Greek lines. The westering sun cast his gigantic shadow back over the massed Greeks and, beyond them, over the beaked ships drawn up on the strand. His shield looked enormous as a chariot wheel. It was made of nine bullhides bound in brass. And he was using Ares' own spear, twenty-feet long, its shaft made of a single ash-tree, which he had picked up after the god of war had dropped it upon being wounded by Diomedes. Ajax was the only mortal large enough to wield this spear.

Hector did not wish to give Ajax a chance to hurl that huge spear, so he cast his own javelin first. It sped through the air and hit Ajax's spear, shattering its brass boss and penetrating all but the last bullhide. Ajax shivered like a tree under the blow of a woodman's axe, but he steadied himself, drew back his knotted arm and hurled Ares' spear. Now Hector was using a smaller shield — also made of bullhide bound in brass. He preferred a shield he could move about to cover himself rather than one to hide behind, because he depended more on speed and agility than size. When he saw the ash-tree lance hurtling through the air toward him he lifted his shield, which was immediately shattered by the spear. His left arm fell to his side, numb. But he swerved his body, avoiding the spearhead, and suffered only a scratch on his shoulder. But that cut spurted blood, and the Trojans groaned.

Ajax did not pose on his followthrough, but let it take him into a wild-boar rush upon his foe — his signature in battle. Hector barely had time to scoop up a boulder. He did not have time to hurl it, only bowled it across the ground. He cast it so skillfully that it took Ajax's legs out from under him, and the big man sprawled on the ground. Then Hector whipped out his sword and rushed toward the fallen Ajax to cut off his head.

Ajax, seeing him come, picked up the boulder which had felled him and, still lying on his back, hurled it at Hector. It hit him on the breastplate and knocked him off his feet. Both men pulled themselves up and stepped toward each other, swords flashing. Blades clanged against breastplate and helmet. Ajax stood still, pivoting, aiming huge scything blows as Hector cir-

65

cled him, half-crouched, darting in and out, using edge and point. Both men were bruised, shaken, and bloody. Neither yet had the advantage.

It was at this point that Apollo intervened — without meaning to. He had not intended to meddle in the fighting. There had always been some coldness between him and father Zeus, and he did not dare defy the high god's orders the way Athena did. So, after his consultation with the owl-goddess, which had resulted in Hector's challenge and Ajax's reply, he had flown off to intercept his sun-chariot, which, in his absence, was being driven by Helios, his charioteer. The sun-god took Helios' place in the chariot, gathered the reins in one hand, and whipped up the fire-maned stallions. They set off in a swinging trot across the blue meadow of the sky, heading toward its western rim.

But when Apollo heard the shouting of Greek and Trojan far below, heard the clang of sword against shield, he dipped lower to watch the fighting. The duel was so exciting, he grew so fascinated that, for the first time in memory, he neglected his duties as the sun's coachman and allowed the stallions to stay in one spot grazing on the fluffy white cloud-blossoms. He kept the chariot reined in, burning a hole in the air, charring the earth below . . . until he smelled something burning. He saw great clouds of smoke pierced by dancing flames where the lingering coach had set forests ablaze. He put his horses to a gallop, leaving that place as quickly as he could, and fled, bright as a comet, toward the stables of night. But the land below had been charred over great distances, making a waste place which, today, men call the Sahara.

His gallop westward had drawn a curtain of night across the earth. Greek and Trojan, amazed, saw the afternoon sun drop like a red-hot coal, hissing, into the sea beyond the western wall of the city. Hector and Ajax groped for each other in darkness.

Heralds bearing long willow wands rushed forth from the Trojan lines and the Greek lines, calling:

"Night! Night! Sudden night! Leave off fighting and seek your tents, for the light has flown."

This was the way they ended battles in those days.

Hector and Ajax stopped fighting. They felt the night wind on their hot brows. All at once, these duelling warriors who had avoided killing each other only by the blunder of a god, felt closer to each other than to anyone else on earth.

"Noble Hector," said Ajax, "I have never met a worthier foe."

"Nor have I, sir," said Hector. "Truly I am glad that the light was so magically brief. I welcome this pause."

"We shall resume tomorrow, no doubt," said Ajax. "In the meantime let us sleep. But, pray, take this as a gift and a remembrance."

He unbuckled a purple belt from about his waist. It was of thick, soft wool embroidered in gold and black with the figures of dolphins that play off Salamis, and do odd favors for men.

"Thank you, great Ajax. It is a beautiful cincture; I shall wear it proudly. But take you this. It has never been yielded, sir, but now it is freely given."

Hector, then, whom a generous gesture always moved to an excess of generosity in return, handed Ajax his silver-hilted sword. The two warriors embraced, turned, and went back to their own lines as the first stars trembled steel-blue in the black sky.

THUNDER ON THE RIGHT

Morning light revealed the battlefield so littered with corpses that Greek and Trojan agreed to a truce so that they might honor their dead, build pyres, offer to the gods, and consign the bodies to decent flame.

That morning, too, Zeus called a council of the gods on Olympus. All the members of the Pantheon were required to attend.

Zeus spoke: "Brothers and sisters, sons and daughters, wife. . . . Many a time have I warned you, gathered here in sacred convocation, and individually to your faces, that I permit no direct intercession on the part of any god in the war below. We may keep our favorites, we may grant godlike dispensations and civilities from the privilege of our godheads, but we are not permitted to descend upon the field and actually handle arms like brawling mortals. Yet, as often as I have issued my edicts, that many times have they been disobeyed.

"Gods . . . I am not accustomed to being disobeyed. The very notion violates not only my principles but my identity. There can be no Zeus where there is defiance of Zeus. You have violated my decrees, some of you, and have intervened on both sides of the battle. Only yesterday my eyes were offended by the unseemly spectacle of brother and sister actually spearing each other on the reeking plain. Do you not know that this is the way that gods destroy themselves? Not by being conquered, not by invasion, through no act of foe, but by stooping beneath themselves — by behaving like mortals. To behave like a mortal is to forfeit immortality. To behave like that animal called man is to forfeit divinity. What is mankind to think when it sees Athena fighting with Ares — in other words, Wisdom in conflict with Warfare? Man seeing this can no longer be either wise or warlike. And since this race of man was created for our edification and amusement, such a falling away from the great creative principles of survival will provide us with an earthful of dull automata whose antics we will find most boring through eternity.

"I repeat my edict then, and for the last time. If I catch any of you, and I mean anyone, no matter who he is or what high domain he rules, if I catch any god or goddess directly aiding either Greek or Trojan, then I shall take that offender and cast him or her down into the depths of hell. Yes, I will plunge that one into the blackness of Hades. There I will fork him with the roots of a mountain, as a boy catches a snake in a cleft stick, so that he cannot budge, but must lie there with giant worms passing in and out of each eye-socket . . . still alive, still possessing all his strength, all his desires, but unable to move, unable to turn or shift, unable to be comforted. And this through eternity. . . . Any questions?"

There was only silence.

Finally, Poseidon, who always stood on his dignity with his brother, Zeus, said: "Really . . . these mortals and their affairs are so petty. So unsavory. I don't see how any god can concern himself overmuch with this breed. Oh, we play favorites, to be sure. I suppose that I tend to prefer the Trojans simply because the Greeks have offended me more in times past. And yet . . . really, to choose between them would be like discriminating among columns of ants as they converge upon a breadcrumb one has shaken from one's board."

Then, casting a sidelong glance at Zeus, he continued:

"Look at them now. Those Greeks are so arrogant and impious. Why they are building their funeral barrows and none of them has thought to sacrifice to Zeus, Lord of Life. Have the Trojans sacrificed to you, brother? Oh, yes, I believe they are doing so now. Aren't those white bulls they are slaughtering? Yes. Well, as I said, little there is to choose between them, yet the Trojans do seem a bit more courteous. But for a god to intercede? Folly. . . ."

Poseidon arose, shook the billows of his green garments, combed his beard with his fingers, and struck three times with his trident upon the marble floor, summoning a tidal wave which curled its awful cold, green tongue over Olympus. He slipped into the cusp of that enormous wave, and upon his command it subsided, rolling him down into the ocean depths where stood his castle of coral and pearl. But the sea-god left behind him, slyly kindled, a wrath in the heart of Zeus, because he had been given the idea that the Greeks had neglected sacrificing to him.

Dismissing the council after his tirade against intervention, Zeus decided to do a little something himself to discomfit the Greeks. He translated himself to Mt. Ida where he had a summer home. He sat on the peak of Ida looking down upon the battlefield. Poseidon's gibe had worked; he was full of rancor against the Greeks. Now Mt. Ida is to the north of Troy, and the Trojans faced westward as they tried to drive the Greeks into the sea, so that when Zeus thundered he thundered from the Trojan right, an ancient sign of good fortune. When Hector heard the thundering, he leaped to his feet and cried:

"Enough of truce, brothers! I hear thunder on the right! Hear it? It is a sign from Zeus; he favors us in the battle to come. So let it begin! To the attack!"

The Trojans armed themselves and began a furious attack upon the Greek positions, driving the Greeks backward upon their ships. Diomedes tried to lead a counterattack, and indeed breached the Trojan lines. His chariot was drawn by the marvellous team of Aeneas, and this get of the sun-stallions was faster than any horses ever foaled. But as he sped toward Hector, spear poised, Zeus spotted him, and hurled his lightning bolt. Thunder crashed. Lightning struck directly in front of Diomedes' chariot. There was an eerie flash, a suffocating smell of sulphur. The horses reared. Diomedes tried to whip them through the smoke, but Zeus threw another thunderbolt. Again the heavens crashed on the Trojans' right flank; again the searing flash of lightning in Diomedes' path; again the sulphur stench. The stallions reared again, whinnying in fright. And Diomedes realized that Zeus had decided to favor the Trojans that day, or that hour. He reined in his steeds and drove back to the Greek lines.

Hector led another savage charge toward the ships. They were protected by a deep ditch, called a fosse. Behind the ditch were earthworks of sand. On top of the sand hummocks, and entrenched behind them, were Greeks. Hector and his brothers began to throw rocks into the fosse, and to throw planks across it, so that they could cross over. Sword in hand they fought their way over their rude bridges and began to climb the earthworks.

Watching from Olympus, Hera cried:

"My Greeks are being defeated! I can't bear the sight of it! Will no god help me? Then I must go alone to save them."

But Apollo said: "No, stepmother, it would not be prudent. Do not tempt the wrath of Zeus. Every word he said to us this morning was freighted with the promise of eternal humiliation and torment for the god who would defy him. I know him well. *You* should know him better. If he sees you crossing the sky in your chariot he will transfix you with a lightning bolt. Alas, I know those lightning bolts; I know how they can kill, for did he not slay two of my sons? You remember Phaeton, who borrowed my sun-chariot, and, careless youthful impetuous driver that he was, drove too high, too low, alternately scorching and freezing the earth. Yes, Zeus toppled him from his chariot with one cast of his fiery spear. And there was some justice to it, I suppose; it is the duty of Zeus to protect his realms. But how cruelly and with what little cause did he send his shaft through my son, Asclepius, the marvellous physician, whose only transgression was that he saved so many of his patients from death that it displeased dark Hades, King of the Underworld, who saw himself being deprived of clients, and complained to his brother, Zeus. And Zeus complied by killing my wonderful son. So, stepmother, I beg you, do not dare that awful wrath. Do not attempt to help the Greeks. It is not their day today. Return to your peak, and abide the question."

Hera was convinced. She returned to her peak and sorrowfully watched the Greeks being routed below. Now the Greeks were driven back upon their ships. If they allowed the Trojans to advance any further, the ships would surely be burned, and with them all hopes of sailing homeward ever again. Agamemnon tried to exhort his men, and his phrasing was as tactless as ever.

"Cowards!" he bellowed. "Empty braggarts. Are you those who claimed one Greek was worth a hundred Trojans? A hundred Trojans? Stand the numbers on their head and we may arrive at something more sensible. For have I not seen one Trojan, Hector, driving a hundred of you at spearpoint like a shepherd dog herding sheep?"

His voice broke into hoarse sobs. Tears streamed from his eyes. He turned his face to the sky, and said: "Oh, father Zeus, why are you punishing me so? Have I not always sacrificed bulls to you, the very finest I could cull from my herd? Great white bulls with black eyes and polished horns and coral nostrils? Swaying broad-backed white oxen too? Or did I per-

72

chance by error neglect some sacrifice or libation to you? Is it for this your hand falls so heavily upon me and my men, delivering us to the enemy? Did not you yourself send me a dream bidding me attack the Trojans, promising me victory? Is this the price of my obedience? Oh, father Zeus, have mercy. Let me at least drive the Trojans a little way from my ships if you can vouchsafe me no greater victory."

Although Zeus was still annoyed at the Greeks and still intent to keep his promise to Thetis that the Greeks would be denied victory until Agamemnon should plead for Achilles' help, still he was touched by the Mycenean king's plea, and he relented a bit. This took the form of fresh courage firing the Greek hearts. Crude as Agamemnon's words were, still the Greeks responded to his speech, and launched a counterattack. They hurled down the plank bridges, and drove the Trojans back from the lip of the fosse.

Teucer now became the most effective of the Hellenes. Hiding behind the enormous shield of his brother, Ajax, he shot arrow after arrow, and it was as if Zeus himself personally guided each shaft. He loosed nine arrows and each one of them killed a man. Nine Trojans fell, nine of the best. With his genius for saying the wrong thing, Agamemnon now rushed up to Teucer, crying:

"Hail, great archer! Every arrow you let fly kills another Trojan. But you must redouble your efforts. Snatch your arrows faster from the quiver. Notch them more speedily to your bowstring, and shoot one after the other without delay. For you must kill as many Trojans as possible while Zeus smiles on you. His smiles are brief, as well we know."

"Why flog a horse that is breaking his wind galloping for you?" said Teucer. "I cannot shoot any faster."

"Certainly you can. You want an inducement. Listen . . . I promise you this. As high king and commander of the forces I pledge that when finally we take and sack Troy you shall have the woman you choose for your very own, no matter how many princes contend for her, and may take your choice from among all the daughters of Priam, and the other beautiful maidens of the court."

"Thank you for nothing," said Teucer. "When we take Troy I'll do my own choosing. Now please, king, break off this discourse, and let me continue to send my bolts into the ranks of the enemy. As we stand here talking they're regrouping. If we linger like this the only thing we'll be taking is a ferry across the Styx."

And, sure enough, by the time he had notched another arrow to his bowstring, Hector had approached close enough to hurl a boulder that caught Teucer square, toppling him, and crushing his collarbone. That would have been the end of the superb little archer except that Diomedes scooped him up into his chariot and galloped with him to safety behind the Greek lines.

This was a turning point again. Zeus felt that he had responded sufficiently to Agamemnon's prayer, and withdrew his favor.

The Trojans crossed the fosse again and forced the Greeks step by step back toward their ships.

Hera, watching on high, was again seized by a savage dissatisfaction, with that imperious burning displeasure that was a hallmark of her character.

"Come, Athena!" she cried. "We must go help the Greeks!"

"No, father Zeus has forbidden it," said Athena.

"My conduct is defined by my neglect of his decrees," said Hera. "Am I a wife for nothing? Forbid it or not, we must go down there or the Greeks are doomed. And after all our efforts! It's intolerable!"

"Be patient but a little while, stepmother," said Athena. "I know that Zeus in the larger measure of things means to abide by his oath of neutrality. He, too, as much as any of us is bound by the anciently woven destiny of the Fates, who are older than the gods, and less changeable. He knows that Troy must fall."

"It will never fall while Trojans are killing Greeks," said Hera.

"Patience, mother. Zeus is but keeping the promise he made to Thetis, the silver-footed, that Greek fortunes would ebb until Agamemnon should be humbled and have to come to Achilles' tent to plead with him to drop his grudge and enter the lists again. When that happens — and the time is drawing near — then Zeus will resume his impartiality and let the Fates work."

"I can't wait that long," said Hera. "Or there will be nothing left down there but Trojans. If you don't join me, I'm going alone."

But Hera had no sooner climbed into her chariot than Zeus made his power felt. Before she had a chance to whip up her horses, swift-winged Iris, the messenger-goddess, flashed across the sky from Mt. Ida where she had been sitting at Zeus' feet awaiting errands.

"Father Zeus is watching you," she said. "He is listening. He sees and hears across great distances. He knows your intentions. And he instructs me to say that if the wheels of your chariot leave this peak you will be transfixed by a thunderbolt — which even now he holds poised, ready to hurl."

Hera threw down her reins and pulled herself from the coach, weeping.

Athena tried to comfort her.

"Take heart, mother," she said. "Night is falling, and the fighting must stop. Perhaps in the watches of the night, father Zeus will relent, and tomorrow turn his favor to the Greeks. Or, perhaps, allow *us* to aid them, if he will not. He is changeable, you know. His moods are brief as they are violent."

Hera, still sobbing, allowed herself to be led into her chamber.

NIGHT

Sentries watching from the walls of Troy were comforted by the sight of a hundred fires burning on the beach. Trojan fires. This meant that the Trojans had penned the Greeks onto a narrow marge between forest and ocean. Hector ranged among the fires exhorting his men.

"Tomorrow!" he cried. "Tomorrow is our day! I feel it in my heart. Tomorrow we will finish what we have begun so well today. We will force them back, back, back upon their ships and slay them every one. We will teach haughty invaders never again to dare the beaches of Troy."

On the Greek side, the scene was much different. Dismay hung like a pall, and no watchfires gleamed. But a solemn conclave was going on in Agamemnon's tent.

"Kings and princes," he said. "Members of the Council . . . I pray your forgiveness. As commander, I must take supreme responsibility for our defeat. And now I ask for your advice. Do you think we should try to save what we can . . . that is, launch our ships under cover of night — this night I mean — and sail for home? Tomorrow, remember, the enemy may cross the ditch and burn our ships, cutting off our retreat. That is the question we must resolve here and now. Do we depart tonight or gird ourselves for tomorrow, knowing that this morrow may be our last among the living?"

Diomedes spoke briefly: "The rest of you can leave, everyone, but I stay. I and my charioteer, Sthelenus. If all the rest of you go, together we will mount the chariot and drive Aeneas' wonderful horses against the Trojans, killing as many as we can, before we are killed in our turn. If you want my real recommendation, Agamemnon, it would be for us to burn the ships ourselves tonight, cutting off our own retreat, and giving every doubter among us the great gift of no alternative. Better to be cut down here like men than to skulk home, defeated, dishonored, disgraced."

"Diomedes, you are a very young man," said Nestor, "but you speak like a sage. Your words are golden, my boy. Golden. I cannot quite hold with you on burning our ships, but this much is sure, we must not sail home tonight. Of course, we must stay and fight. And, by the gods, if we face the enemy without dismay, we will win. For the Fates have foretold it. And their decree not even the gods may alter. But I have this to say: We must decide on a very important step tonight. By this I mean we must coax Achilles back into the fold. Agamemnon, the burden is yours. You must apologize to him and make amends, and I know how this will torment your proud spirit. But you have no choice, truly. You must take upon yourself that humiliation; must eat your arrogant words, return the slave girl you took from him, and give him rich compensation besides. Then, perhaps, we can persuade him to fight tomorrow. My Lord Agamemnon, this is absolutely necessary. Without Achilles we are just an army; with him we are an irresistible force."

Agamemnon spoke: "Honorable Nestor, dear sage, adept councillor, I speak no word in objection. I will humble my spirit and do everything necessary to persuade Achilles to join our ranks once again. I was wrong to quarrel with him, wrong to take the tall Briseis . . . wrong, wrong, wrong! I can ascribe my actions only to some hostile god addling my wits, and doing us more harm thereby than if he had supplied the Trojans with a company of slingers, a company of archers, and a cavalry troop. Now I have come to my senses again. Harsh defeat has restored my balance. I see how misguided I was — and this is what I propose to do for Achilles if he consents to stand beside us tomorrow. Hark now to my gifts of appeasement. First, cooking ware, rich enough to prepare a feast for the gods: seven bronze kettles, twenty huge pots of burnished copper, each of them big enough to boil an ox in. Ten gold ingots, each of them weighing almost a hundred pounds. Six teams of matched stallions that in a chariot race would press the sunbred stallions of Aeneas. Seven girl slaves, the most beautiful of all those captured in nine years of island raiding, all of them contortionists, and very good at embroidery too. Lastly, I shall return to him tall Briseis — and with her my oath that she comes back into his hands untouched by me.

"Generous? Yes. But this is only the start, good sirs. When we return to Greece I shall bestow upon him other gifts, beyond the dream of avarice. I shall consider him my son, an elder brother to Orestes, with all the privileges appertaining to a prince royal in Mycenae. He will choose a wife from among my two beautiful daughters; her dowry will be seven cities, the richest in the land. I pray you, inform Achilles of my offer, and bring me his answer."

"Very well," said Nestor. "And on behalf of the War Council let me thank you for the remarkable generosity you now display. I have no doubt it will make Achilles forget the insults he suffered at your hands. I propose that the overtures be made to him by the men he respects most: Phoenix his old tutor, Ulysses, and Ajax. And I myself will accompany these three, for, in all modesty, he esteems me also."

When the delegation came to the tent of Achilles they found a very peaceful scene. There was a driftwood fire burning, and the smell of roasting meat. Achilles was playing a silver-chased lyre and singing a boar-hunt song of Phthia. Patroclus lay back listening dreamily. Achilles sprang to his feet when he saw his guests. He embraced them, calling to Patroclus:

"See, my friend, how we are honored. Our companions, battle-weary, come to visit us instead of refreshing themselves with sleep."

"Oh, son of Peleus," said Patroclus. "I believe you misread their intent. They come not to exchange amenities, nor pass the time; not even to indulge themselves in your warm hospitality. They come on business, grim business. Am I right, friends?"

"Your wits have always been as sharp as your sword, good Patroclus," said Ulysses, "and, unlike your sword, have been given no chance to grow rusty. Yes, we come on business. Grim business. Survival is always a grim affair. And it is particularly grim when your enemies have you penned on a narrow stretch of beach threatening to slaughter you like cattle and burn your ships."

"Business or not, grim or not," boomed Achilles, "nevertheless we shall preserve the amenities. You have come on a visit to my tent, and it is my custom to feed visitors. Patroclus, will you do the honors of the table, sir?"

Patroculus served the savory roast meat and the rich purple wine. Greedily, the guests fell to. Agamemnon had neglected to feed them at the Council. When they had fed, Achilles said: "Now, sirs, say to me what you will. I am all attention."

Then Ulysses, always the spokesman in any delegation, told Achilles how greatly Agamemnon desired to make amends, and the rich gifts he was offering.

Achilles answered, saying: "If anything could persuade me to drop my feud with Agamemnon and join battle against the Trojans, it would not be his bribes, but the feelings of comradeship, respect, and affection I have for you, great Ulysses — and you Ajax, you Nestor, and you, Phoenix, beloved friend and mentor. Nevertheless my answer must be no. I loathe and despise Agamemnon. In open meeting before all the troops, he insulted me repeatedly; spoke to me as if I were the seediest of camp-followers. He laid rude hands upon Briseis and dragged her away. So, my friends, when you report back to him, tell him to keep his cook-pots and his ingots and his talented slave girls and his seven cities in Mycenae. As for his kind offer to wed me to one of his daughters, I can say only this: I have not met either of the two young ladies. I hope for their own sakes they resemble their mother Clytemnestra, or their aunt Helen. Nevertheless, heredity is a quirky thing. Lineaments and traits of personality have been known to skip generations. Ask my lord Agamemnon if he thinks I would risk having a son or daughter with his pig face and verminous disposition. No, gentlemen. The answer is no. Tomorrow, at dawn, my Myrmidons and I board our ships and sail away to Phthia. Patroclus comes with me. And you, Phoenix, old teacher, do not stay and sacrifice yourself in this vain war, but come on board my ship and sail home with me."

Phoenix could not speak; his voice was strangled with tears. He simply nodded to Achilles, and embraced Nestor and Ulysses and Ajax in farewell. They said not a word in protest, knowing it would be futile, but took courteous leave of Achilles, and left his tent.

ON THE WALL

It was as though the gods, heavy with business, had pressed the sky low that night between battles. The stars hung low, pulsing, each one big as a moon; the moon itself was a golden brooch pinning the folds of darkness that were night's cloak. The gleaming watchfires on the field looked like star-images dancing in water; standing on the west wall it was hard to tell where the sea ended and the beach began. Under the immense jewelry of the summer night lay the corpses of the day's fighting: bodies pierced and broken; smashed heads of beautiful young men; severed arms and legs. They bulked strangely now; they were heaped shadows. Pools of blood stank and glistened in the moonlight. Birds came down to drink.

The night is beautiful on the Dardanian plain when the sky

81

presses low, flaunting its jewelry. A night not to sleep in, though you be battle-weary, or love-weary, or devilled by hope, or torn by fear. On both sides of the fosse men seethed restlessly. Men and women still lingered on the walls of Troy where they had watched the battle all day. Usually, by night, the walls were bare of all save sentries, but this night pressed with too many hot lights; people trying to sleep were pressed between flaming sky and reeking earth, and were tormented by dreams that drove them from sleep.

Helen and Cressida lingered on the wall. They were wrapped in long cloaks; their faces glimmered in the weird light.

"I have been wanting to talk to you," said Cressida.

"Indeed?" said Helen, frowning slightly.

She was the daughter of kings and the wife of a king, paramour of a prince, and was being fought for by all the kings of Greece. She was proud. And Cressida was only a priest's daughter — but recently a slave in Agamemnon's tent. The difference was great between them.

"Forgive me for addressing you so familiarly, Queen Helen," said Cressida in her odd furry voice. "I know the distance between us. But, you know, you are a heroine, a demi-goddess. When you go out on the streets of Troy not only princes admire, but the populace cheers itself hoarse too. I am not too humble to esteem you. And, being here on the wall with you this way, after a day of such sights, I cannot forbear from addressing you. There is something old in our hearts that tells us wisdom is allied to beauty. And I need wise counsel."

"Nay, put aside these ceremonial forms of address," said Helen, reaching her long arm and putting her hand on Cressida's shoulder. "We are two women together." For admiration was soul's food to Helen, and the clever words of Cressida fired her vanity and made her ignore social distinctions.

"Two women together," murmured Cressida. "Yes. And we have watched the battle all day. With what mixed feelings women watch. Men are lucky; they're so simple; their alternatives are so crude. Kill or be killed. Good or bad. Noble or cowardly. Their simplicity is what gives them power over us, O Queen of Sparta. For we are poor weak divided creatures, torn by distinctions. We see our loved ones fighting, and we want them home safe. Yet, if they kill — and they must kill or be killed — it is other beautiful young men they are destroying. It is a waste. And waste is what women cannot abide. We hate to see things thrown out while there is still use in them. And there was use in those young bodies, glorious hot-blooded use. Forgive my babbling, Queen, but I am more affected than others, I suppose, because, as you know, I lived among the Greeks. There were no strangers to me today on either side of the fighting."

"You forget," said Helen. "I, too, know Trojan and Greek."

"It is different with you now, beautiful queen. For your heart and soul reside in that radiant young prince, Paris. And you must whole-heartedly follow his fortunes. . . ."

A strange voice broke in.

"But will she follow her prince to Hades — where he must soon go by reason of her foul enticements?"

It was Cassandra. Almost invisible because she was clothed in black, but her eyes, like a cat's, were burning holes in the darkness.

"You know my little sister-in-law, no doubt," said Helen. "And do not feel offended. What would be the most unpardonable rudeness in anyone else is genius in her. The sign of genius, apparently, is a systematic and ruthless discourtesy."

"You have good reason to dislike me," said Cassandra. "The moment I saw you I knew you meant the destruction of Troy. Every breath you exhale poisons Ilium. Every glitter of your leman's eye kindles a flame for that night of flame when Troy will be sacked. In your voice that coo of love is the death-rattle of brave men."

"You see how wise one is in accepting flattery when it comes," said Helen to Cressida. "So soon afterward one hears something else."

"Good Cassandra," said Cressida. "On such a night, between battles, when the darkness itself seems pregnant with events struggling to be born, on such a night, there is an appetite, I think, for prophecy more than for food or drink or love. Tell us what will happen — who will be killed tomorrow and who survive? Will the Trojans drive the Greeks to the sea and burn their ships? Will the Greeks drive back the Trojans and storm these walls? Will Achilles return to the fray? Will Hector rage again like a lion in the field? And what of Paris? And young Troilus — so like Paris in beauty of face and form, yet shy where his brother is bold — what of him? He escaped death by a hairbreadth today; will he be as fortunate tomorrow?"

Helen was gazing at the moon, seemingly absent, but listening hard all the same. For she recognized in these last words of Cressida not an address to Cassandra but a message to herself. Cressida fancied young Troilus among all the Trojan men, and was obliquely asking Helen to drop a hint to the lad, the most naïve and inexperienced of all Priam's fifty sons.

"Do not plague me with your sordid little queries," said Cassandra to Cressida. "You say one thing but mean another. You seek to entrap my brother, Troilus."

"I do not understand what you mean, dear Cassandra," murmured Cressida. "But then it is said that you often prophesy in riddles. Are you doing that now — riddling us? Please tell us what will happen in the battle tomorrow. But in plain words."

"In plain words, shut up," said Cassandra. "I will not speak of the battle tomorrow. I will not speak at all. But wait. I do see something. A bloody thing is about to happen right now. Not tomorrow, *now*. My vision, god-poisoned, pierces distance. I see Ulysses and Diomedes preparing for a foray."

"Diomedes," said Cressida. "A very likely man. He was another Achilles in the field today. He seemed like a god descended, bright as a star. I've never seen anything like it."

"Yes," said Helen. "He is too young to have been one of my suitors. Today I rather regretted it. He put on a remarkable performance. Remarkable."

Cassandra went on: "Ulysses dons a skullcap of boarhide

and a half cloak of polished boarhide to serve as an arrow-proof vest. Diomedes, despite the warmth of the night, wraps himself in a wolfskin cloak. They costume themselves like this to cast bulky shadows, for the moon is very bright, and they wish to steal among our men — and Ulysses is a master of artifice. They carry short hunting spears, and knives at their belts — no swords to rattle against their legs. No bows and arrows, for they will be working in close. They seek to raid our lines and capture a Trojan and extract information from him. And into the jaws of this trap the gods are sending one of our officers named Dolon. He seeks to invoke the aid of darkness by putting on a moleskin cloak and moleskin cap. For moles are blind and cannot see, and their hide, he believes, will protect him from being seen as he scouts out the Greek positions. Foolishness. The whole art of magic is the exchange of attributes through invocation, and he has no magic. Poor Dolon . . . he must die."

Cassandra paused. Unwinkingly her cat's eyes burned holes in the darkness.

"Tell . . . tell. . . ." whispered Helen. "What are they doing? Please tell. . . ."

Cassandra resumed her tale in a low monotonous voice. She cared nothing for her listeners — she never cared for listeners — she told things to herself, but she knew that others overheard. "The Greeks pick their way among fallen bodies and pools of blood. At their approach, birds flutter away. When they pass by, the birds return to drink. There is a rustling as rats scurry amid the corpses. Oh, things of night do feed richly upon the battle's fruit."

She fell silent again and the others, listening, thought they heard rats gnawing and birds sipping. And these tiny sounds were the most terrible they had ever heard.

"Listen well, my slothful sisters, and I will tell you a tale of this busy night . . . of this vast and starry bloody night. Ulysses and Diomedes pick their way among corpses to spy upon the Trojan lines, while Dolon skirts pools of blood to spy upon the Greeks. They will meet, they will meet, and sad will be the tale thereof. For Dolon knows a secret. Upon this night allies have come to join our forces. King Rhesus of Thrace with a thousand henchmen — from that land behind the north wind where men grow large and fierce. Drawing the chariot of King Rhesus is a pair of horses unmatched by any in the world except those that Diomedes took from Aeneas earlier today — a pair of milk-white mares, sired by Pegasus upon one of the white-maned gray mares that draws Poseidon's chariot when he raids the beaches.

"And their coming should be a joy to us. O Watchers upon the Wall, sisters, the coming of Rhesus should be an occasion for rejoicing. For anciently it has been told that our city cannot fall once these mares drink of our river. Once these thirsty steeds dip their muzzles into the waters of the Scamander and drink therefrom, the walls of Troy must stand and its inhabitants be undisturbed. Will Rhesus arise in the rose and pearl dawn of the Dardanian plain? Will he start the bronze dust as he drives his chariot toward the Scamander and allows his mares to drink before the thirsty work of battle begins? Alas, alas, Dolon knows that the Thracians have come with Rhesus at their head. He knows they guard the right flank, that they have put out no sentries, and that they sleep soundly after their exhausting journey. He knows the tale of the prophecy. Dolon steps quietly. But Ulysses has ears like a fox; he hears someone coming. He pulls Diomedes into the shade of a tamarisk tree, and there they wait. They seize Dolon when he comes. Yes . . . now they have him. He has fallen into their jaws like a mole taken by a night-running hound. They tie him to the bole of the tamarisk tree. He pleads with them; they do not answer, but speak to each other in grunts. Now he is ready. Ulysses takes out his knife, saying: 'We are Greeks. We are after information. You will please answer what we ask or we will carve you like a joint of meat. You are dead already, you see, because we will not leave you alive. But you can spare yourself some pain. Why not spend your last minutes without pain?'

"Dolon sobs. He is a brave man, but not brave enough for this. He is brave in the sunlight, but now they are under the cold lamp of the moon. He has been ambushed by shadows, by men big as shadows who speak to him in a strange yet understandable language, saying nightmare things.

"Diomedes grows impatient while Dolon hesitates. He wields his knife and slices a finger off Dolon's hand. Dolon's screams are stifled by Ulysses' hand clapped over his mouth.

" 'That hurts, does it?' says Diomedes. 'Don't forget you have ten of those, not to mention your toes. Why don't you tell us what we want to know?'

"Dolon cannot bear this; few men could. He begins to babble away telling them more than they wish to know. Ulysses slaps him across the face, bidding him be still and just answer the questions.

" 'Have you posted sentries?'

" 'No.'

" 'Why not?'

" 'We thought you were too beaten, too disheartened to make any forays this night.'

" 'How are you encamped? What are the disposition of your forces?'

" 'We Trojans hold the center. To the left, toward the sea, lie the Lelegians, the Cauconians. On the left flank are those raiders from Crete, the sea-harassing Pelasgians. To the right of us are stationed the Lycians, the Mysians, the Phrygians and Maeonians. On the extreme right flank are those newcomers, the Thracians, under King Rhesus.'

" 'The Thracians? Are you sure?' said Ulysses. 'I know of no Thracians here.'

" 'They have joined us only tonight. I was a member of the welcoming party. Pray let me go, good sirs. My father is the herald, Eumedes, and heralds grow rich in times of war. He will pay a large ransom for me. I will tell you what I know, but then let me go.'

"Diomedes prods him with the point of his dagger.

" 'Speak on,' he says. "Who leads these Thracians?'

" 'I told you, King Rhesus.'

" 'Is he accounted a good fighter, this Rhesus?'

" 'The finest. Ranks with the best. And, in a chariot, is perhaps the very best. For his steeds are matchless.'

" 'Indeed?' asks Diomedes. 'Better than those of Aeneas?'

" 'As good, as good. Some say better. They were sired by Pegasus upon one of Poseidon's own surf-mares. They are tall and they run like the wind. And his chariot is made of silver and gold with brass wheels — and his axis sprouts six long knives which scythe down the enemy. Am I not a good informant, O captors? Pray, accept a ransom and let me go.'

" 'But how many men does he lead?'

" 'A thousand Thracians come with him. But best of all . . . I know something else! Don't kill me yet, don't kill me yet! I have something else to tell!'

" 'Tell away. The night grows old, and our patience short.'

" 'Don't kill me yet, not yet! Just listen to this!' "

Cassandra broke off her tale, eyes huge and staring.

"Go on . . . go on," cried Helen.

"Don't stop now . . . Tell. Please tell," whispered Cressida.

"Oh, no!" muttered Cassandra to herself, pressing her knuckles against her mouth. "He must not! No, Dolon, do not tell them! Do not inform them of the prophecy! It will be fatal! . . . Oh, coward! He tells! He tells! . . ."

"Tells what?" cried Helen.

"What I told you, you fat-hipped fool! Has it fled your memory so soon? The prophecy concerning the mares of Rhesus — that if they drink of the Scamander's waters, Troy shall not fall. He tells this to Diomedes and Ulysses; that is all they have to know. Ulysses thanks him and signals to Diomedes who, with one swift movement, cuts Dolon's throat as if he were a sheep. They leave him bound to the tamarisk tree, and set off to their left — toward the extreme right flank of our lines — where sleep Rhesus, the Thracian host, and the fatal mares."

POSEIDON
DECIDES

The god of the sea was vexed. Unlike the other gods he had held himself aloof from this war. He had preened himself on being so far above the affairs of petty mortals that he might not stoop to take a hand in their quarrels. This was a unique position in the Pantheon; all the other gods had lined up one way or the other. And, for a while, this sense of uniqueness served his pride. But now of late he had felt a difference. The combatants, Trojan and Greek, offered him fewer prayers, less sacrifices, adorned his statues more meagerly, built him fewer altars. They implored his intercession only in specific sea matters — voyages, piracies, and the like. But this had developed into a land war, so Poseidon was feeling neglected.

"All because of my impartiality," he raged to himself. "An attribute I have always held truly divine. Instead of being thankful that I do not meddle in their battles, killing this one, saving that one, turning all their plans awry — instead of being thankful for my benign indifference, they have dared to neglect *me*. The Trojans, knowing that Athena is against them, sacrifice to her constantly. But yesterday Hector sent all the women of Troy in great droves, led by Hecuba, to the Palladium to pray to Athena to turn a less furious face upon them. Similarly, the Hellenes court Apollo, who favors the Trojans. Yes, they pray and sacrifice to him and to his cold sister, and to that blundering bully, Ares. They crawl to all the gods who favor Troy. The Trojans again fill the air with supplications to Hera, whom they know loathes them. It's getting so a god has to punish a nation to get its respect. Well, I'm weary of being neglected. I shall take sides too. Those I favor shall thank me, those I mistreat shall implore me. . . . Yes, I shall have my mede of mortal attention — without which, it is curious to say, we gods, even the most powerful of us, are apt to shrivel and waste.

"Now who shall it be — Trojan or Greek? Very difficult. No instantaneous bias suggests itself, only a mild dislike for each."

The trouble here was that Poseidon for all his tempestuous bluster had a strong feminine side to his nature. He was incapable of loving or hating people in groups. Generalization irked him. He could form a powerful attachment to an individual — as he had to Theseus, for instance, said to have been his son — and keep an eye on him through all circumstance and crown his deeds with glory. Or, far more often, he could hold an implacable grudge against someone, and pursue him with storm, tidal wave, sea-monster, every type of marine catastrophe. But, as he thought about things, he found himself incapable of preferring either Greek or Trojan en masse.

"Let's see," he said. "Let me consider this carefully. Certainly I can find cause to favor one side or the other. . . .

"Greek or Trojan, Trojan or Greek? Shall I have to draw straws? Seems a paltry device to decide such potent favor.

Perhaps I should consult my preferences among the gods — who have all involved themselves in this fray. Here again it is very difficult. I have reason to dislike all my brothers and sisters, nieces and nephews. My sister, Demeter, has always pleased me the most, I suppose. On the other hand, she takes least interest in this war among all the Pantheon. She dislikes war too much. It means the destruction of crops, whoever wins. And she is the Lady of Growing Things.

"I have this old feud with Athena, and her espousal of the Greeks might lead me to choose the Trojans. Against this, though, those mealy mouthed, high-stepping twins, Apollo and Artemis, help Troy, and I should not wish to be on the same side of any question as they are. Apollo's flaming nuisance of a chariot parches my waters whenever it can catch them in shallow pools. While that grasping, bare-thighed, male-hating icicle sister of his has the gall to meddle with my tides. Her keen whistle pierces to the underwater kennels where the seadogs sleep. She summons them, leashes them with a chain of silver light, and swings them high, low, despite my dominion of the sea. Her I will destroy one day. I don't quite know how, but I will find a way.

"Difficult . . . most difficult question. Quite gives me a headache."

And he spit a tidal wave that covered an ancient island with a wall of water a hundred feet high. When the wave subsided the island had disappeared, and has never been seen since.

All this time he had been hovering over the face of the waters. Now he whistled up his chariot — not the beach-raiding one drawn by his white-maned gray mares, but the sleek green sea-going chariot drawn by dolphins. He sped to his palace of coral and pearl. Seated on his great throne, which was of whalebone lined with mother-of-pearl, he felt more at ease, and resumed his thought.

"I am unable to decide this way," he said to himself. "That is clear. Perhaps it is better so. Weighing this, calculating thus, that has never been my style. My rage is storm. My kindness a fall of light, sudden bliss of blue weather. I am sudden, capricious, king of tempest. The sea itself takes its famous changableness from my moods. I shall watch the battle then as it shapes up this morning and, as I watch, take inspiration from what I see. Yes . . . that will relieve me of this head-splitting meditation, and provide some diversion also. For I find uncertainty pleasing — and have always diced with dead men's bones. Very well, then, I shall watch the battle, and decide. And woe be to the forces, Greek or Trojan, whom I decide against."

He took a great bowl made from a single chrysoprase, the largest in all the world. It is a light-green jewel pure as a child's eye holding much light. This bowl of chrysoprase he filled with clear water. And, watching the water, and thinking about the Dardanian plain, he saw cloudy pictures form and dissolve, and they were the images of battle.

Poseidon, like all gods, was intensely amused by the sight of men fighting. The fiercer the fighting, the more he enjoyed it. A good killing sent him into peals of laughter. This laughter of the gods at the sight of death and suffering is sometimes dimly heard by men — as a natural sound, usually, the wind howling on a peculiar note, the cry of an owl striking, a scream out of nowhere waking the sleeper who tries to identify it, and fails.

Thus, Poseidon, on his whalebone and nacre throne, rocked with laughter as he saw the battle rage on the Dardanian plain. He saw the cloudy images form and dissolve in his bowl of pure water. So much blood was spilled in these scenes that the bowl was tinged with red, and this pleased Poseidon.

He saw Agamemnon, clad in gorgeous armor, goaded to fury by the whisper of Athena. Agamemnon clove the Trojan ranks, thrusting with his long spear, shearing through shield, breastplate, helmet — crushing bone, drinking blood.

"How gaudy he is, this commander," said Poseidon to himself. "This wild boar from Mycenae who cannot utter a word without creating dissension; how splendidly he is clad, and how splendidly he fights, to be sure. Marvellous his armor. Of lapis lazuli, of bronze, and of pure beaten tin. He glitters like a beetle on the dusty plain. And, like a beetle, he can be crushed."

Just as Poseidon said these words the picture in the green bowl dissolved from that of Agamemnon spearing the elder son of Antenor, to a picture of the younger son of Antenor spearing Agamemnon. The younger son, Choön, drove his spear through the king's shoulder. Agamemnon's counterthrust pierced the lad's eye-socket, and split his skull. But Agamemnon, bleeding sorely, was forced from the field.

Grinning, Poseidon signalled to a naiad, who took up the bowl and poured out the blood-tinged water, and refilled it with clean water and returned it to the laughing god. Now Poseidon, conning the waters in the bowl, saw Hector rally the Trojans for a counterattack that carried them back over the field half-way to the fosse.

Here at the lip of the fosse the best of the Greeks took a stand against the Trojan's hurricane charge. Diomedes flung a rock at Hector that crushed the crest of his helmet and hurled him to earth, stunned. But Aeneas straddled the fallen Hector and covered him with his shield, and Diomedes could not follow up his advantage. Such was the fever of combat burning in Hector that his dizziness fled, and he sprang to his feet, ready to fight again. As Diomedes hesitated, seeking a way to get at Hector, Paris slithered near. Sheltering behind a tree, he notched an arrow to his bowstring, and let fly. It was a splendid shot. Had he ventured closer before shooting he would have killed Diomedes, but the tree was a long bowshot away, and the arrow struck downward, piercing Diomedes' foot, pinning it to the ground. Seeing that Diomedes could not get at him, Paris laughed, and came closer, fitting another arrow to his string.

"It was you, was it, prince of sneaks!" roared Diomedes. "Hiding behind a tree like a mountain bandit, and shooting arrows at your betters. Miserable ambusher! Puling abductor! Dare to come within my reach. Dare to meet me with spear or sword!"

Diomedes stooped and pulled the arrow out of his foot despite the awful pain of the barb tearing backward through his flesh. Paris was so disconcerted at this stoic feat that he melted into the crowd again without shooting his second arrow. But Diomedes had lost much blood; he had to quit the battle.

Now Hector, flanked by Troilus and Aeneas, swept like a brushfire along the bank of the Scamander where the Thessalians were making a stand.

Paris had hastened to join this group because he preferred to shelter himself behind an impenetrable hedge of such shields. But he was welcome. His archery was inspired. It was as if Apollo himself had tutored him in bowmanship between one day's fighting and the next. Every arrow he shot found its target in Greek flesh. He sent a shaft through the shoulder of Machaon, who fell where he stood. A shout of despair arose from the Thessalians. Machaon was their king; not only their king, but the most able healer in the Greek camp. Son of Aesclepius himself, he had been taught by the great surgeon, and had mastered his father's art. This made him a grandson of Apollo, of course, but he had lost Apollo's favor by fighting on the wrong side.

It was old Nestor who leaped out of his chariot and lifted the fallen Machaon, and drove him safely back to the Greek lines. But the Thessalians were disheartened by the loss of their leader and would have crumbled before the Trojan charge had not Great Ajax come rushing up, and rallied their wavering ranks with a loud war-cry.

All this time Poseidon was watching the battle in the visionary waters of his bowl. Octopi wrestled beyond the huge windows set in his palace of coral and pearl. Sharks glided, smiling their hunger. Shoals of long-legged naiads swam by, hair floating. Balloon-fish, giant rays, the artful twisted glyph, the only sea-creature that can outmaneuver an eel. All the rich traffic of the sea swam past his window — which he so loved in his ordinary hours, but which he failed to notice now, absorbed as he was in the shifting images of battle.

He saw Ajax standing among the broken Thessalians, steady as a rock, with streams of Trojans dividing upon him as waves break upon a rock. The Thessalians gave ground; the Trojans swarmed. Ajax, for all his huge strength, was about to be over-whelmed. Then Poseidon's heart bounded with pleasure as he saw Ulysses storm up in a chariot drawn by a pair of magnificent mares. Milk-white they were with black manes and brass hooves.

"How did Ulysses come by that team?" said Poseidon to himself. "They belong to Rhesus. They are the get of my own surf-mares, sired upon them by Pegasus. But he could not be driving them, and Rhesus alive. What could have happened?"

He shook the waters in the bowl until they darkened into images of the night before. He saw Ulysses and Diomedes, act-ing upon the information they had tortured out of Dolon, steal into the Thracian lines, cut the throats of Rhesus and twelve companions, leap into his chariot and whip up the beautiful steeds to a windlike rush back beyond the fosse.

"So that's how they did it," said Poseidon to himself. "What devils they are, those two — crafty, bold, imaginative, ruthless. How can the Trojans possibly stand against such men; how could they have withstood them for nine years? Zeus secretly helps the Trojans; that's the only explanation. Despite his oath of neutrality he is sending signs and portents to hearten the Dardanians beyond the limits of their own mortal strength. And yet he threatens with awful punishment any of the other gods who intercede."

Poseidon shook the waters in the bowl again, and returned to the day's fighting. Ajax and Ulysses, shields locked, were making a stand on the banks of the Scamander. But they had each suffered wounds, and, step by step, were being forced back. Finally, Ulysses grasped Ajax, who was more seriously wounded, about his waist, thick as the trunk of a tree, and with an enormous effort hauled the giant into his chariot. Then he whipped up the white mares, who galloped so fast it seemed they were flying. With one bound they leaped the Scamander, pulling the chariot through the air after them, and sped behind the Greek lines.

But now the Trojans were free to ford the river, storm the fosse, break the ramparts, and burn the ships. With the flight of Ulysses and Ajax, with Agamemnon, Diomedes, and Machaon wounded — and Achilles still refusing to fight — the battle had definitely turned in favor of the Trojans.

But now Poseidon had decided. He could not retrace the process by which he had made the decision — but he recognized an enormous urgent partiality toward the Greeks. He lost no time. He sent a message by a naiad who swam underwater to a marg of the Inner Sea where a river cuts its way to the shore. There the naiad rose to the surface and sang a summoning song, which was answered by a nereid, a river nymph. She arose, tall, naked, brown-haired, and dripping, to meet her green-haired cousin. The naiad whispered the message to the nereid who swam upstream to the source of the river — a spring on the slope of the mountain. She arose from the water, sleek as an otter, and sang a summoning song. A song answered — far and coming near. Running over the fields came a troop of dryads or wood-nymphs. The nereid spoke to their leader, a tall, black-haired nymph with suave satiny muscles tightening her brown skin.

"I will bear the message, cousin," cried the dryad, laughing.

She ran up the slope again, followed by her troop, screaming and laughing. The nereid watched them until they disappeared into a grove of trees, then dived back into the river and floated downstream. The tall dryad ran to a certain grove on the slope of Olympus where she knew Hera was wont to hunt. There she found the goddess holding a hooded falcon on her wrist, instructing it — which she did quite fluently. She was queen of the air and spoke the language of falcons and of all birds. The dryad knelt before her.

"A message from Poseidon, oh queen."

"What have you to do with Poseidon, hussy?" cried Hera, who, like her falcon, would not be in good humor until their first kill. "Has he been hunting on these slopes again? Does he not have naiads aplenty that he must seek my dryads of the Sacred Grove? Why, he's as insatiable as his elder brother, if that is possible."

"Pardon me, queen," said the Dryad. "But I was not given this message by him, personally. It was brought by a nereid who swam upstream from the Inner Sea — and she had it from a naiad sent by the Lord of the Deep with this message to be given to you, and you alone."

"What is it?"

"He wishes to meet with you on a matter of much urgency. He will meet you halfway on the isle of Patmos."

"Urgent for him or for me?"

"A most important affair," he said, "which he could confide to your ear alone, but that you would rejoice to hear."

"Thank you then for the message," said Hera.

She uncinched the falcon from her wrist, and gave it to the dryad.

"Take him back to the palace for me. Catch a rabbit and feed it to him, fur and all. But take care of your fingers."

Hera whistled. A chariot appeared, drawn by eagles. She mounted the chariot, uttered a piercing eagle scream, and sped away off the mountain toward the blue puddle of the sea.

Poseidon's residence on Patmos was a great cave. He received Hera very courteously.

"Sister, forgive me for bringing you this distance. Had I come to visit you on Olympus, the wrong ear might have heard us speak, and a tattling tongue borne our business to Zeus."

"Ah, this is to be a secret from Zeus then," said Hera.

"A heavy secret. Heavy enough to crush us both . . . if we are not prudent. I have observed, sister, that your husband has broken his oath of neutrality in this war between Trojan and Greek, and has now tipped the balance in favor of the Trojans . . . though their numbers be fewer and their heroes less splendid. So I, who abhor dishonest dealing, have resolved to abandon my own posture of impartiality — by which, you know, I have truly abided, alone among the gods — and to cast my influence on the side of the Greeks, whom, I know, you favor also."

"That is well known," said Hera. "At the moment it's not helping them much, but I haven't played out my string yet."

"Precisely," said Poseidon. "And now I give you a new melody to play on that string. A most seductive one."

"Speak plainly, sir. I do not like this deep-sea riddling."

"Plain as plain, gentle Hera. I mean to intervene actively in the battle, for there is no time to waste. The Trojans have crossed the fosse, are about to burst through the rampart, and drive the Greeks into the sea, thus ending the war. I mean to visit that beach myself, and tip the battle the other way. But Zeus must not see me do this. Else he will hurl his thunderbolt, nail me to the indifferent earth with a shaft of light, then send his Titans to drag me to Hades and chain me to the roots of a mountain, in awful blackness, in choking dryness, there to abide for that endless, sleepless night called eternity."

"And you dare to defy him like this? Knowing the penalties? Truly, this is a change of heart, brother of the deep."

"It is that, high sister. And the success of my venture depends, as I said, on his remaining ignorant of what I am doing."

"How will he remain ignorant? He sits on his peak on Olympus, or a more private one on Mt. Ida, and studies the battle below with keen and vigilant eye. If you even approach the Dardanian plain he will see you."

"Then we must get him off that peak, sister. We must close that keen and vigilant eye. And of all the creatures on earth, of air, or in the sea, mortal or immortal, you are the one to do this. For you are the most beautiful, the most sumptuous, the most regal, the most intoxicatingly seductive personage in all creation. You must woo him off his mountain, hold him tight, and beguile him with such delights that he will forget the bat-

98

tle below. This will give me time to help the Greeks."

"I never realized you thought me so attractive," said Hera. "We have known each other since one generation past the beginning of time, and never have you looked upon me with ardent eye, or spoken such words."

"The modesty of a younger brother. I knew you were destined for our elder brother, who was to be king of the gods and deserved the best."

"Well, it's a dangerous, dangerous game," said Hera. "Old Zeus is a male, true. And, like all males, vulnerable to a low blow. Nevertheless, he is very wise, very cynical, very mistrustful, very difficult to deceive for any length of time. However, I find you oddly persuasive this hot afternoon, and I will try to do as you ask."

"Trying is not enough; you must succeed," said Poseidon. "Don't forget, you were the first to espouse the Greek cause, and have kept it alive these nine years, you and Athena, against all the stubborn resistance of your husband."

"That is true. I hate Paris, loathe the Trojans, dote on the Greeks. And, suddenly, dote on you, dear Poseidon. So I shall return to Olympus and do what you want done."

"It is just before the noonday meal," said Poseidon. "Would it not be better to approach him after he has dined? Like all males he has difficulty managing more than one appetite at a time. This gives us an hour or more."

"Gives us an hour or more for what?"

"For rehearsal, sweet sister."

"You are full of ideas today, my wet lord. One of them better than the next. . . ."

HERA AND ZEUS

       Poseidon was sleepy after Hera left, and would have much preferred to nap the afternoon away in the flowery grove on Patmos. But he knew that the Trojans were pressing hard, and that he must act immediately. He mounted his chariot and hastened to Troy.

Down on the field the Trojans had crossed the fosse and were storming the rampart, which they were trying to knock down with battering rams. A squad of them lifted a log and rushed toward the wall at a dead run, smashing it against the wooden palisade. The timbers groaned and shuddered, but still stood. The Greeks were thrusting down with their long lances from the top of the rampart. At each battering-ram charge the Trojans were losing men. Then Zeus sent a sign. He swerved an eagle in its path so that it crossed the sky to the right of

Hector, and dipping closer to the beach than eagles ever fly. And Hector knew that the god of air and mountain had sent the eagle as a sign.

Filled with joyous strength at this signal of divine favor, the Trojan leader now did something no man had ever done before. He ran to a wrecked chariot; with a mighty heave pulled off one of its wheels. Then, as Greek and Trojan watched him in disbelief, he lofted the enormous copper-spoked brass wheel, and whirled as if he were hurling a discus. The wheel flew on a flat trajectory like a discus well-thrown, and struck the rampart beyond the fosse, knocking a huge hole in it. Hector uttered a loud war-cry and charged toward the gap in the wall followed by his men. They crossed the fosse, climbed up the other side through a cloud of darts and arrows, then rushed toward the breached wall, still following Hector who was several paces ahead, his brass helmet flashing light.

It was then that Poseidon came to the beach. All in gold he came, in a golden chariot, wearing golden armor, carrying a golden lance.

"Too soon, too soon," he said to himself. "Hera will not have had time to woo brother Zeus from his vigil. If I appear like this he will see me and hurl his thunderbolt. Yet, if I delay, the Trojans will overrun the Greek camp. I must act now — but in disguise — and let us hope that Hera on her part does not delay; or that her husband is not immune to her wiles. For Zeus sees quickly through disguises."

Poseidon then put on the form of Calchas, the Greek soothsayer, and appeared on the other side of the rampart among the Hellenes. He stationed himself near great Ajax, and faced Hector, who, with the eagle-rage still upon him, face and body glowing like a demi-god, was charging the center of the Greek line, held by Great Ajax, Little Ajax, and Teucer.

Hera had not been wasting time. She knew how desperate the situation was. But, for all her haste, she made careful preparation. She knew that after a thousand years of marriage Zeus found her charms something less than irresistible. His changeableness in these matters had become a fact of nature, and indeed had produced a large variety of demi-gods and heroes. But Hera was ferocious in her moods too, had a volcanic temper, and time had never made her accept the ways of Zeus. So they had bickered down the ages with increasing rancor and, for the last few centuries, had seldom been together. Therefore, she fully understood how difficult was the assignment given her by Poseidon. She visited Aphrodite, and said:

"We have quarreled, cousin, but I think it is time to forgive each other. I will forgive you for having so shamelessly suborned Paris' judgment and forced him to award you the golden apple as the most beautiful of us all. It is done now, and cannot be undone. It will not change. But I will forgive *you* if you will forgive *me* for all I have done and said against you, and for my ardent espousal of the Greek cause — which also will not change."

Now Aphrodite had a passive easygoing nature, especially in the summer. She was quick-tempered and vengeful like all the gods, but did not have the patience for feuds. Besides, she feared Hera.

"Queen Hera," she said, "you could not have uttered words to give me more pleasure. Long have I wearied of this quarrel between us. I apologize for any harm I may have done you and, with a full heart, forgive you for any injury you may have done me."

The two goddesses embraced, but not too closely.

"Since we're friends again," said Hera. "I am emboldened to ask you a favor."

"Ask away. I am sure the answer will be yes."

"Will you lend me your girdle — that magic garment which arouses desire in any man or god you fancy?"

"Girdle? I wear no girdle. Look at me."

She pirouetted before Hera.

"Do I look like I'm wearing a girdle, O queen? And what would I do with such a thing after my charms work on this man or god? It would just get in the way."

Hera frowned. "Come now," she said. "Don't trifle with me. Everyone has heard about your magic girdle."

"That which everyone knows is most likely to be wrong," said Aphrodite. "I deny that any such girdle exists. What you refer to is simply the essence of those attributes which make me Goddess of Love and Beauty. Do not forget that I can make myself irresistible, as you say, not only to any man I fancy, or any god — but that my favor, extended to any other female creature, makes *her* irresistible to any god or man *she* fancies."

"Are you going to help me? Yes or no?"

"Yes, yes, yes. . . . Let me prepare you for love, and no man or god will resist you, no matter what his inclinations are. Once I have scented you with the distilled attar of those flowers in whose amorous cups bees linger longest; once I have kneaded into your flesh my secret ointment which makes any hag as sleek and supple as a sixteen-year-old girl, then you can approach what god or man you will, and know that in two winks of an eye he will be grovelling before you."

"Sounds promising," said Hera. "I place myself in your hands."

Poseidon had not dared to exert his full efforts in helping the Greeks until Hera had been given time enough to distract Zeus. What he did was stand as close as possible to the center of the Greek line where Great Ajax held the field, aided by his brother, Teucer, and Little Ajax. There, disguised as Calchas the soothsayer, Poseidon flung his arms heavenward and pretended to raise his voice in prophecy, crying:

"Great Ajax, Little Ajax, Teucer the archer: stand fast, stand fast. Resist the Trojans, and you will finally prevail. For a great god is coming to aid you, a great god I cannot name seeks your victory. He cannot come yet, but he will come and cover you with his mantle, and you will be invincible. So stand fast, stand fast."

The three warriors, heartened beyond their own knowledge

by the keen gull-cry of the pretended Calchas, fought more savagely than ever and held back the Greek advance.

Hera flew to Mt. Ida, to its tallest peak, Gargarus, where Zeus sat watching the battle unfold.

"Greetings, dear lord and husband," she cried. "Forgive me for breaking upon your solitude, but I am departing on a long journey and did not wish to leave without saying good-bye."

"Where are you going?" said Zeus without turning around.

"Off to the bitter margin of the earth where our uncle, Oceanus, and his wife, Tethys, reside. Lately it has come to my notice that they live in terrible loneliness with each other, keeping a cold distance between them because of some ancient quarrel, never exchanging a kind word, never dining together, nor warming each other with a caress. I go to reconcile them so they can live together again as man and wife."

"Who do you think you are, Aphrodite?" said Zeus. "Lovers' quarrels, reconciliations. She takes care of all that."

Hera came very close to him.

"But I am moved by pity for my Aunt Tethys," she murmured. And in her voice was the song of birds. "I know what it means to be denied a husband's caress. To long for him with all my heart and soul and to be denied, denied. . . ."

Zeus turned, then. Hera was very close to him. She gave off a powerful fragrance of sunshine and crushed grass.

"Besides," she whispered. "Aphrodite has lent me her bag of tricks. Has tutored me in certain arts that are bound to reconcile that stupid feuding man and wife."

By this time Zeus was completely enraptured by the sight of his wife, who looked as beautiful to him as she had when the world was very new and they had hid from their parents, old Cronus and Rhea, wrapping themselves in a cloud and loving each other with such hunger that the cloud had burst and the valley of Olympus was flooded. And Cronus and Rhea had been forced to give permission for the brother and sister to wed. He stood up and clasped her in his arms.

104

"Before you trundle off to the ends of the earth," he said, "there are a husband and wife here who have some arrears to make up."

"Right here?" she whispered. "Here on the highest peak of Ida? But all the Pantheon will see us. I am proud, proud to be loving you again my lord, but such revels as I plan are better done in privacy."

"Privacy we shall have," said Zeus. "Without moving from this spot."

Thereupon he caused the rock to grow anemones and roses and hyacinths and sweet grasses to a height of three feet, making a soft bed. And he pulled down a fleecy cloud to cover them like a quilt, quite concealing them from view, shielding them from the sun with a delicious moistness, bathing them with the lightest of dews.

And the folk who lived in the village at the foot of the mountain felt the solid rock shake, saw their slopes tremble, heard the giant sounds of Zeus' pleasure. And they fled their village thinking their mountain had turned volcanic and was about to erupt.

As Hera lay down with Zeus she released a dove which she had been carrying on her wrist like a falcon — a swift-darting, blue and gray bird specially trained to bear messages and keep secrets. It darted to earth, and found Poseidon where he stood on the Trojan beach disguised as Calchas. The bird cooed to him, relating Hera's message that he could help the Greeks as much as he liked because Zeus would be too busy for the rest of the afternoon to notice what was happening on earth.

ATTACK AND COUNTERATTACK

Bellowing and dancing in his exultance, the Lord of the Deep cast off the guise of old Calchas like a tall tree twisting in the wind shedding leaves. He made himself invisible, all except his golden trident, and when he wielded the great three-tined staff it was like the sun-fighting clouds sending spears of light through the cover. Invisibly he approached Great Ajax and Little Ajax and Teucer and goaded them with his trident. A great salt wave of health broke upon their blood, filling them with the surging strength that the god of the sea can bestow. They led their men forward in a mighty rolling charge that smashed against the Trojan line like the ocean sending its white-plumed breakers to pound a foundering ship. And the Trojans, who had been so triumphantly victorious just a few moments before, now began to retreat.

106

Hector went purple in the face with rage, smacking his men with the flat of his sword, trying to harry them forward. Ajax, knowing his strength multiplied, stooped to pick up an enormous boulder lying half-buried in the sand — a massive rock, seemingly rooted in the beach — which twelve men had been unable to move. He raised it above his head with an easy motion and hurled it straight at Hector. It hit the Trojan hero's shield, driving the shield against his chest, knocking him flat. He seemed to be crushed like a beetle; he lay under the rock, legs kicking feebly. But then with a last indomitable effort he thrust himself from under the boulder, and lay there, unable to rise, vomiting blood. Aeneas it was who lifted him onto his shoulders and rushed back toward Troy. Prince Troilus covered their flight, fighting like a young lion.

But when Hector left the field, the Trojans were shattered. The retreat was becoming a rout. By this time Poseidon had ranged behind the Greek lines where the wounded leaders stood in a cluster watching the battle. Agmemnon was there, Diomedes, and Ulysses. Patroclus was there too, tending their wounds. The comrade of Achilles was the most skilled surgeon among the Hellenes. Poseidon, keeping himself invisible, spoke to them in sea-whispers. A huge salt wave of health broke upon their blood, healing them, knitting bone, mending flesh. With loud, glad cries they leaped into their chariots and lent such strength to the Greek countercharge that the Trojans were driven back through the breach of the rampart, scrambling back over the fosse. Troilus tried to make a stand, so did Antenor, and a few other of the most redoubtable Trojan warriors, but they could not stem the Greeks alone, and finally had to flee after the Trojan force which had fled before.

Bedded on flowers and sweet grass, wrapped in a fleecy cloud, Zeus slept in Hera's arms; and everywhere, except on the Dardanian plain where the battle wore on, lovers touched each other in sleepy rapture. Everywhere, over field and meadow, hung a haze of pollen thickening to a golden drift under the slant rays of the afternoon sun — so that lovers mov-

107

ing toward each other through the grass felt themselves cleaving a heavier substance than air, felt their very blood fusing into a golden heat.

But on the Dardanian plain men killed each other. Heavy metal blades cracked bone, sheared through flesh. Beautiful young men, naked under their armor, drowned in their own blood. And still the Greeks pursued and Trojans fled.

High upon Mt. Ida, on a peak called Gargarus, Zeus slept in Hera's arms. But Hera did not sleep. Drowsy though she was, still her interest in earthly affairs kept her from joining her husband in slumber. Which turned out to be a mistake. . . .

Moving very carefully, very slowly, she slipped out of his embrace, slithered out from between flower bed and cloud cover, and walked to the edge of the precipice. She looked down upon the Dardanian plain. What she saw made her forget her caution and laugh aloud in triumph. The Trojans were in full flight, pursued by furiously yelling Greeks whose swords and spearheads dripped with blood.

With Hector gone, Paris fled, Troilus and Aeneas wounded, the Trojans were a disorganized rabble instead of an army. It appeared as though the Greeks might be able to storm the walls of Troy there and then. Again Hera laughed.

Too loudly! She heard Zeus grumble. She had thought him deep asleep. She whirled about. To her horror she saw him sit up, stretch, yawn — and scratch his monumental chest. She ran to him and knelt upon the flower-bed, stroking his shoulders.

"Do not awake, dear lord!" she murmured. "Sleep, sleep."

But Zeus stood up. The habit of vigilance was strong upon him. Besides, into the depths of his sleep had wound a skein of mocking laughter. He put her aside gently and walked to the edge of the precipice.

"Don't look down there!" she cried. "Why trouble yourself with mundane affairs? Rest, rest, great lord of creation! The rusty old earth will turn a few turns without you."

But Zeus was looking down upon the plain. His huge brow

was furrowed like striated rock. He whirled and took Hera's throat in those enormous hands that crack stars like peanuts.

"Things have changed," he said softly. "since we two lay down together. I left the Trojans ascendant. They had breached the rampart and were driving toward the Greek ships. And now, what do I find? Poseidon down there, my treacherous brother, who has turned the tide of battle so that the Greeks are everywhere triumphant. Tell me, was it coincidence, sweet sister, steadfast wife? Was our sudden encounter after all these centuries one of those happy accidents? Or perhaps part of a deeper design?"

"I can scarcely follow what you are saying," said Hera. "Poseidon at Troy? The Greeks winning? But this is a very abrupt change — as surprising to me as it is to you. What can Poseidon be thinking of to defy your edicts this way? It's dreadful."

"Be still! Don't try to play with me. I am very angry."

"Angry at me? Do you so soon forget the delicious hour we spent?"

"No, I do not forget. And I may even look forward to other such hours — unless, of course, I decide to punish you so painfully that you will seek to avoid my company. However, we can postpone that decision. Let me attend to Poseidon first."

The God of the Sea stood tall in his golden armor just beyond the beach, balancing himself on the surf like a child on a skateboard. From time to time he uttered a great northwind yell to hearten the Greeks. But matters were going so well now, he had little to do but watch the battle. Suddenly the sky growled. He looked up. No storm clouds at all, but a wide fair expanse of blueness.

Out of the blue sky shot a thunderbolt — a hooked shaft of white-hot light, burning the air as it passed. It plunged into the water, just missing Poseidon, immediately turning the sea to steam.

"What are you doing?" cried Hera, pleading with Zeus above. "Are you trying to destroy your own brother, Poseidon, Lord of the Deep? Think of the consequences."

"He should have thought of the consequences," growled Zeus. "I *am* consequence."

"Consider his record," pleaded Hera. "He may have transgressed a bit this afternoon, but after all up until now he has been the most neutral of the gods in this war, has been the one who has obeyed your edicts most strictly."

"That is why my first bolt missed," said Zeus. "As you know I usually hit what I aim at. I hope it serves as a warning. For my second bolt will not miss; it will gaff him like a fish."

But there was no need for another bolt. When Poseidon saw the white-hot zigzag shaft of lightning hit the water he was bathed in steam; felt that he was being boiled like a lobster. And he knew that Zeus had seen him, and was angry. Pausing only to flick a quick idea at Ulysses, he uttered a whistle, which evoked his dolphin chariot in the wink of an eye. Instantly he had mounted the chariot, and was gone — down, down into the depths of the cool sea where all the creatures are too busy eating each other to bother about such things as war.

Poseidon's last idea flew like a dart and hit Ulysses painlessly in the neck, passing into his head, nestling just beneath his consciousness ready to sprout as a full-fledged idea when its time should come.

"I cannot tell whether you are guilty or innocent," said Zeus to Hera. "Perhaps I do not want to know. It is the essence of a beautiful woman that she bewilder — and in this a goddess is as a woman — so let it be. But do nothing from now on to change my opinion of your innocence. In other words, dear wife, keep your meddling hands off that war below, or I'll cut them off."

"Yes, husband," murmured Hera.

"Now fly back to Olympus and send Apollo to me. We must undo the harm you have done. Let him come immediately."

Hera was frightened. She did not take the time to fly but translated herself back to Olympus where she said to her stepson, Apollo:

110

"Go . . . go. . . . Go swiftly to Zeus. He awaits you on Mt. Ida, on the peak called Gargarus. He wants you immediately."

Apollo appeared before Zeus, who said: "That briny uncle of yours has played us false. He has appeared among the Greeks, endowing them with such strength and courage that they are about to overwhelm the Trojans. I suspend my act of neutrality now — or at least amend it — so that we may be neutral on the Trojan side. Go to work, dear Phoebus. Rally the Trojans. Make them fight again, and prevail."

Now, Apollo, of course, had watched that afternoon's fighting, and had been much impressed by the feat of Hector with the chariot wheel. He took a spare wheel of his sun-chariot, one of those glittering golden disks, that, trundling across the blue meadow of the sky, refract the eternal fire as they turn, flashing; and that fire falls to earth in a benign glow that men call sunshine. He took this heavy glittering wheel, and, holding it as a shield, flew to earth.

He appeared among the Trojans, flashing his sun-shield at them and kindling their courage, burning away fears and hesitations. He went to where Hector lay on a litter, pale and crushed and unconscious, almost dead from the blow of Ajax's boulder. Apollo focussed light upon the fallen hero who, in the clammy grip of his swoon, felt the cockles of his heart warming, felt his every vessel filling with sap, putting forth buds. The amazed Trojans saw Hector arise, flushed with heat, eyes glittering.

"What are we doing here?" he cried in a voice like a trumpet. "Why here, in the shadow of our walls? For shame! For shame! The last I remember we were beyond the rampart, advancing upon the Greek ships, ready to put them to the torch. And now, and now. . . . How could we have retreated so far? So soon?"

Troilus spoke. He had refused to be carried beyond the walls for treatment despite grievous wounds.

"I'm with you, brother!" he cried. "Both my arms are broken, but I can still lower my head and charge like a stag."

Aeneas, also wounded, said: "A breath ago we were gripped by despair, ready to yield the city. And now — such a change! It is obvious, good friends, that a god is among us, that we have again earned the support of heaven, which we had lost for a bitter interval this afternoon. But the favor of gods abides only among the brave. So, forward under Hector! Forward! Forward!"

"Each prince to his chariot!" shouted Hector. "We will mount a chariot charge, one such as our fathers mounted in days of old, and still lie about."

Now, the Greeks, who had been enjoying themselves chasing the Trojan rabble across the field and spearing them like rabbits, found everything changed. Instead of a fleeing mob scurrying toward Troy, they saw a rank of bright chariots rushing toward them with terrible speed. They heard the squeal of wheel against axle, heard the clank of weapons, and the bugling neigh of the chariot-steeds, and their eyes were assailed by splintering light. They saw light gathered in their enemy; light in sheaves, in quivers, in darts and lances; light splintering off breastplate and helmet, and brass wheel and brass coach, and the brass corselets of the chariot-horses. Light that splintered, quivered, danced; refracted by Apollo's sun-shield — which, keeping himself invisible, Apollo wielded behind the Trojan lines, harrying them forward with bright cries. And the Greeks, seeing these phalanxes of light, hearing the bright trampling triumph of the chariot charge, knew indeed that the god who had been helping them had deserted the field and that a god who loved their enemy had descended in his stead. They turned and fled. Fled from the shadow of the city wall over the corpse-littered field, in their fearful haste stepping on the bodies of men fallen, not caring whether they were friend or foe.

Back the Greeks swarmed, back over the field, scrambled across the fosse, streamed through the breach in the rampart, and took a stand only when they had reached the first line of ships. The Trojans, doubtless, would have stormed through and begun to burn the ships had it not been for the superb courage of Great Ajax, Ulysses, Diomedes, and Agamemnon, who kept their heads through all the dismay of the route, and rallied their men to beat the Trojans back from the ships.

Great Ajax sprang on board his own ship. He snatched up his thirty-foot mast from where it nested in its cradle on deck, and flourished the enormous shaft as if it were a light throwing lance. He swept it over the gunwales of his ship breaking Trojan skulls like eggs, helmets and all, and swept the deck clear.

Then it was that the glinting dart of Poseidon's last idea which he had planted in Ulysses' head began to flower. Ulysses, close-hemmed between Diomedes and Little Ajax and locking shields with both, suddenly whispered to them: "Dear comrades, I quit you only on a matter of strategy. Lock your shields."

He backed away, took the shields of Little Ajax and Diomedes in his hands, and lapped them with each other, and no gap appeared in the line. He then simply walked away from the battle, walked toward the tent of Achilles which stood with the Myrmidon fleet at the other end of the beach.

"This is it!" he said to himself. "A master notion. Achilles still sulks in his tent ignoring our mortal peril, the death of his comrades, the humiliation of Greek arms, and the certain destruction of the fleet. But he is still nourished by that poison pride of his, and by his justified rancor against Agamemnon, and he still refuses to fight. Nevertheless, suppose his dear friend, Patroclus, were to impersonate him? Don his armor, wield his weapons, ride his chariot, and lead his Myrmidons into the field? That would be a superb stroke. One of two things must happen: Either the Trojans will believe that Patroclus is Achilles, and, seeing him, flee in terror, as they always have; or, they will see through the disguise and kill him. Then, if Patroclus falls, Achilles will have to choose between two passions — his pride and his love for his friend. And, I am sure, with his dear friend fallen, that great heart will burst with spleen, and he will take arms and sweep the field like plague. Either way we can't lose. All I have to do is persuade Patroclus to talk Achilles into lending him arms and armor."

Achilles' tent was cool after the hot sun. And the young warrior, seeing Ulysses so battleworn, refused to let him say a word of business until a slave girl had been summoned to loosen his armor, bathe his feet, swab his face and neck with a cool scented cloth, and bring him a restorative drink of barley steeped in honey.

"Thank you, great Achilles," said Ulysses. "As all men know, your courtesy is equalled only by your courage . . . by the memory of your courage, that is. For indeed no man has seen you recently performing those feats of arms which made you famed among the famous before you were old enough to grow a beard."

"Your conversation is always stimulating, friend Ulysses. The gloss of your compliments always conceals a sharp-edged gibe. But you are, as usual, justified. I know that I have been a noncombatant recently, know it well. Do you not think that I chafe at this inactivity? I am like a tiger playing with a ball of wool, hearing a lion roar as he hunts my deer. My desire for battle is so fierce I feel that I could drink blood by the goblet . . . like some ancient ogre who ate men raw. But I am bound by an oath never to fight on this field as long as Agamemnon leads the Greeks. So I must abide here in my tent, listening to the sounds of battle, being beguiled by my beloved friend, Patroclus — and, occasionally, having the honor of entertaining such fighters as you."

"A truce to compliments," said Ulysses. "I have not come here to urge you to fight. In the past few days you have been begged to do so in more eloquent phrases than I can lay tongue to. No, I come with another suggestion: that you, Patroclus, play Achilles. We need an Achilles, even a counterfeit one. And what more fitting than that you, friend of his heart, should put on his armor, take his weapons, mount his

114

chariot, and lead his Myrmidons in a charge against the Trojans?"

"Ridiculous!" said Achilles.

Patroclus said nothing.

"Perhaps you don't appreciate the gravity of our situation," said Ulysses. "We are at our last gasp. Even now the Trojans would be firing our fleet did not Great Ajax, like a Titan of old, fight them off with a mast he is using as a spear, carving a place for himself in the history of arms that will never fade as long as men love courage. But when Ajax falls, as fall he must, then they will burn the fleet, not excepting your own ships unless you set sail immediately. Yes, they will put our proud beaked ships to the shame of the torch, and then, in all leisure, penning us between fire and sea, will slaughter us like cattle. You refuse to fight, Achilles. Very well. You are bound by an oath, fettered in your pride. You will not fight. But, in the name of all the gods, lend us your shadow. Allow Patroclus to impersonate you. It is our only chance."

"What do you say, Patroclus?" said Achilles. "Do you wish to do this thing?"

"I do," said Patroclus.

"Then you shall. I will be your squire, and dress you myself in my own armor that I never thought any other man should wear."

"Thank you, great Achilles," said Ulysses. "Thank you, gallant Patroclus. I must hasten back to the fighting now. Even the whisper of what is to come, I'm sure, will hearten our comrades so that they can withstand the Trojans yet a little while — until Patroclus shall appear on the field."

PATROCLUS

Patroclus stripped himself then in Achilles' tent, and put on his friend's armor. Achilles acted as squire, helping him don corselet, breastplate, greaves, and plumed helmet.

"Beloved friend," said Achilles. "I wish I could clothe you in my invulnerability instead of these pieces of metal. Oh, they are beautiful pieces of metal, cast of molten gold, and brass, with inlay of copper and tin, made by Hephaestus himself as a wedding present for my father, Peleus. The enemy, seeing this armor, know that it is Achilles they must face, and are disarmed by fear before they can begin to fight. But, friend, let me tell you a secret that no man knows, and no woman either, except my mother, Thetis. I can fight without that armor, and

116

no spear, no sword, nor arrow can pierce me. For my mother, queen of the nereids, ranks as a goddess, and she wished to give me, her son, sired by a mortal, her own immortality. So, when I was just nine days old she dipped me into the River Styx, that black stream that separates the land of the living from the land of the dead and whose waters have magic power. Every part of me the water touched was rendered beyond hurt — tough as nine layers of polished bullhide, stiffened with brass — without losing the delicacy of human skin. Thus, no blade can cut me, no wound kill. All except one place."

Achilles lifted his foot and tapped the great tendon over his heel.

"She held me right here as she dipped me into the river. Where her fingers clasped, the waters could not touch. In this one spot I am vulnerable."

Patroclus laughed. "Not an easy spot for an enemy to reach," he said. "To expose it you would have to be running away. And that is a sight no man has ever seen, or ever will."

Achilles laughed, and embraced his friend.

"Truly," he said, "you are a gallant fellow. Here you are about to meet the Trojans — in the full exultant tide of their victory, when their courage burns hot, and they fight better than they know how — and you are smiling and jesting as though you were at a banquet."

"Dear friend," said Patroclus. "Clad in your armor I feel as safe as though I were at a banquet, reclining on a couch, being served wine by the slave girls and chatting with the other guests. As Ulysses said, clad in your armor I go forth as your shadow, and even the shadow of you, mighty warrior that you are, is enough to chase the Trojans the best day they ever saw."

"One word of advice," said Achilles. "You will be followed by my Myrmidons, who, having been kept out of battle, are rested and fresh. They will give a good account of themselves. The Trojans should break before you. But please, I implore you, when they break, do not pursue them. Let them retreat in their own way. If you follow them, keep with your troops. Do not charge ahead. Do not seek to despoil a fallen foe of his armor, no matter how rich it is. Above all, do not seek single combat. The Trojan heroes will not be seeking an encounter with you, either, clad as you are, so such duels should be easy to avoid. Avoid them! Most important of all, do not seek to engage Hector in hand-to-hand conflict. Now go, dear Patroclus. And may the fickle gods go with you."

He embraced him again, led him to his chariot and helped him mount, then walked quickly away to the edge of the tide, and stood there looking out over the sea. For his heart was heavy with foreboding.

Patroclus, shining like the morning star in Achilles' armor, vaulted gaily into Achilles' chariot. It was of burnished bronze, drawn by a pair of stallions named Xanthus and Balius. They were of divine breed. Their dam was not a mare at all, but a harpy named Podarge who had become amorous of the West Wind. She foaled, dropping two colts, matched blacks with golden eyes, silver hooves, mane and tail of silver fleece. They ran as swiftly as their sire, the West Wind; in their temperaments was the loving ferocity of their dam, Podarge. They were loving to their master, but savage in battle. Achilles had trained them to rear back and strike like a boxer with their silver hooves; one blow of a hoof could crack a warrior's helmet like a nutshell. They used their great yellow teeth also, snapping like crocodiles. No man dared handle them except Achilles and Patroclus. Achilles boasted of their intelligence, saying they could speak if they wished, but preferred to remain silent.

Drawn by these stallions and driven by Patroclus, the burnished bronze chariot of Achilles whirled into battle.

The Trojans were still trying to burn Ajax's ship. Hector had mounted the deck where the giant still wielded his thirty-foot mast. Ajax swept the deck with the huge staff, trying to crush Hector. But each time the mast swept toward him Hector either ducked beneath it or leaped above it. Each time he did this he struck at it with his sword, each time hacking off a piece

118

of it, until Ajax was left holding only the fat stump of the mast, which he hurled at the Trojans, who were again swarming over the gunwales, killing two of them. Then Great Ajax leaped off the deck, and tried to rally his men for another stand.

Gleefully the Trojans set Ajax's ship to the torch, and began to fire the other ships of the first line. Hector pressed forward swiftly after Ajax, wanting to finish him off — so swiftly that he became separated from his men. Suddenly he heard the shouts of triumph change to cries of bawling fear.

"Achilles! It's Achilles! Flee! Flee!"

He turned, and saw his men break and flee before a chariot of burnished bronze drawn by those stallions he recognized as Xanthus and Balius. Riding the chariot was a tall figure in golden armor, his crest a plume of eagle feathers. Hector's men, chased by the bright chariot, were like a swarm of field mice and hares fleeing a grass fire. Brave Hector himself was sucked up in the wind of that going, and fled before that chariot to the walls of Troy.

Patroclus, riding in his bronze car, felt the armor of Achilles clinging as lightly and intimately to him as his own skin. Yes, it was as if by some stroke of the gods he had been given a hide of supple bright armor, had been fanged with glittering blades, and had come among the Trojans terrible as a tiger among deer.

He swerved his chariot toward where the enemy was thickest. They fled before him always; they could not outrun his stallions. He scythed down the Trojans like summer grass. Everywhere he led, his Myrmidons followed — wheeling, charging, moving like one man.

They followed after Patroclus at a dead run. No matter how fast the chariot was drawn by those stallions sired by the West Wind the Myrmidons would always catch up, and engage the Trojans at the point where Patroclus had broken their lines.

Hector stood on a low hill under the west wall of Troy watching his men flee. It was here that he meant to rally them

119

to try to prevent the Greeks from storming the wall. But he was full of foreboding. He did not see how he could put any heart into his terror-stricken men. Then he smelled a sunny fragrance and heard a voice full of angry music. He dropped to his knees to listen to the words of Apollo.

"I am disappointed in you, Hector. You were my chosen hero, the man of men who was to combat Achilles. Throughout this war you have plumed yourself on being the only Trojan who would dare to close with the son of Peleus. And now what do I see? You flee his shadow."

Tears streamed down Hector's face. He felt himself burning with shame. He could not answer.

"Yes, his *shadow*," said Apollo. "And I mean it not as a figure of speech, but literally. For that glittering armor clothes not Achilles, but Patroclus, who has borrowed his mighty friend's appearance, knowing that it alone would be enough to frighten the Trojans into fits. For almost ten years now I have been trying to warm you with my own flame. I see it is hopeless. No one can help cowards; they defeat themselves. I am going to stop defying my father, Zeus, and keep aloof from this war."

"No, bright Phoebus, no," pleaded Hector. "Do not withdraw your hand from us. Lord of the moving sun, I pray you— lord of the harp, of the golden bow, heed my plea. I will prove to you I'm no coward. I faltered for a moment, it's true, but if you abide with me, I will reclaim my manhood, and straightway engage Patroclus. And when I do, he is a dead man. I further swear that when Achilles comes to avenge the dead Patroclus, as come he must, I will not fear to meet him either, but will challenge him to mortal combat."

Then the sun-god appeared in all his radiance before Hector, and said: "Rise, Hector. Rise, and reclaim your manhood."

Apollo took off his golden helmet whose crest was a plume of red and blue flame.

"Dip your spearpoint into this plume of flame," he said. "And go, hot-handed, to meet your false foe."

Hector arose and held his spearhead in the plume of flame that sprouted from Apollo's helmet. The god became invisible again, leaving only his fragrance behind — the odor of oranges and roses and those fruits and flowers that love the sun. This fragrance enrapt Hector, filling him with a wild exultance. Yelling his war-cry, he rushed toward Patroclus, shouting: "Actor! Mountebank! Fraud! Descend from that borrowed chariot and fight in your own name."

Patroclus heard this bright cry, and wheeled his chariot about. He remembered Achilles' warning, that on no account was he to seek out Hector in single combat. But by now the mask had grown into the face: Aping Achilles, triumphing like Achilles, he had *become* Achilles — or so he thought. Often in days past had he and Achilles felt close enough to have been joined by a membrane, like a pair of unnatural twins, one bloodstream coursing through both bodies. So now he leaped from his chariot, and rushed toward Hector, shouting:

"Well met, son of Priam! Whether I be Achilles or Patroclus, you will never know the difference because the same blade will find your heart."

He ran so fast that he outraced the Myrmidons. Hector raced to meet him. They met with a crash of weapons like two stags breaking their antlers against each other. Brave he was, Patroclus, and fair. Nobly he wore Achilles' armor and handled Achilles' weapons. But he was no Achilles. And Hector at that moment, burning with Apollo's flame, was more than Hector.

Patroclus never had a chance. Swiftly, delicately, Hector handled his spear. The white-hot spearhead sheared through Patroclus' armor like a welding torch — for Hector wished not only to vanquish Patroclus but to ease the pain of his own shame by shaming his foe.

Greeks and Trojans watching this duel saw a sight never seen before. Hector's white-hot spear cut through Achilles' armor; corselet, breastplate, and greaves dropped off Patroclus, leaving him naked except for his helmet. He hurled his spear.

121

Hector laughed as it rebounded from his shield and leisurely advanced on his naked foe.

"You look like a plucked chick, little Patroclus," he jeered. "If I were cruel as a Greek, I would stand here, using my sword like a butcher's knife, and joint you like a chicken. But such is not my purpose. I have bared you this way so that all men may see that it takes more than armor to make a man. Now, actor, it is time for your death scene."

With an upward stroke he speared Patroclus through the belly. It was a bad death. Patroclus fell, screaming horribly, clutching at his entrails.

ARMOR FOR ACHILLES

Patroclus sprawled in the bloody dust. Hector lifted his voice above the battle din.

"Take the body, men! Bear it to Troy! I shall set his head on a pike on the city wall, so that Achilles may meet his friend again, face to face, if he seeks to storm the wall. As for the body, we shall throw it to the dogs!"

But before the Trojans could seize the body, Menelaus rushed up and straddled it, growling like a mastiff, fighting off everyone who approached. Other Trojans pressed forward; other Greeks pressed in to aid Menelaus. A bloody battle raged over the corpse.

What happened to the dead, in those days, was very important to the living. Bodies were not buried; they were cremated. The flames were made sacred by sacrifice to the gods, by libation, and by prayer. In the case of a great warrior, or a king, or

123

of any person who had earned unusual respect during his lifetime, the death ceremonies would include funeral games — chariot races, wrestling, boxing, spear-throwing and archery — reflecting in play form the mourned one's aptitudes in manly pursuits. By such ceremonies and celebrations, it was felt, the dead person could depart in all honor; this sense of honor would ease his journey to the Land of the Dead and give him status in Hades' kingdom. If sufficiently honored at his funeral, he would be singled out from among death's hordes by Charon, the grim boatman whose job it was to ferry them across the Styx. The honored one would not have to linger in a mob, sorrowfully, on this side of the Styx, but be ferried quickly over by the status-conscious Charon to his reward in the land of the dead.

On the other hand, if, for some reason, a corpse went unclaimed by friend or relative — or was kept by the enemy and not given a proper sendoff — then dreadful things would happen to the survivors. The dishonored dead could not cross the Styx and enter Hades' kingdom. His spirit would cling to the site of his unregarded death. Wearing stinking rags of flesh he would appear before family and friends, usually at night, howling, weeping, begging. Or, worst of all, he would be found standing in any hidden corner, staring at you out of empty eye-sockets. If you were unfortunate enough to have dealings with a ghost, you would set out his favorite food — black beans in little pots, shallow dishes of blood — and he would be appeased for a while by such delicacies. But not for long. Soon he would reappear, howling, begging, or silently staring.

In the case of the Greeks, demoralized as they were at this point of the battle, they still fought savagely for Patroclus' body, because they knew that Achilles would go berserk when he learned of his friend's death. But if Achilles also learned that the body of his beloved companion had been taken by the Trojans, beheaded, and then thrown to the dogs, they knew he would be capable of doing anything — to friend as well as foe. In fact, it was probable he would visit his first vengeance upon the Greeks.

124

Thus, despite being outnumbered by the Trojans, they formed a hedge of spears around the body, and would not let the Trojans pass.

But Hector sent in more men, and the weight of their numbers must finally have broken the Greek resistance had it not been for Achilles' horses, those magically bred stallions, tall as stags and fierce as Harpies. They charged toward the knot of fighting men, burst into their midst, and hurled people in all directions. Rearing on their haunches, they struck with their front hooves, kicking and biting until they had cleared the Trojans away from the corpse. This allowed Menelaus time to lift the body and put it in the chariot. Then the horses galloped back toward Achilles' tent, bearing their dead charioteer.

Patroclus had come very close to the Trojan wall before being killed and so the fighting had been beyond Achilles' sight, although he had been watching from the rampart trying to follow the course of battle. All he could hear was faroff shouting; all he could see was a cloud of dust.

"Under their walls," he said softly to himself. "I told him not to advance so far. Still, perhaps it means that he has broken their lines, and put them to flight."

Then he saw a bright speck detach itself from the dust and fly toward him. He watched until it took shape. A chariot! Coming with such speed it could be drawn only by Xanthus and Balius, his own stallions! His heart leaped with joy.

"It's Patroclus!" he cried. "It must be he! They will obey only his hand beside mine! He's safe! Safe! Coming to report a great victory!"

With incredible speed the West Wind stallions galloped to the rampart, rearing and neighing when they saw Achilles there. He looked at them in amazement. Great tears were welling from their golden eyes. No one had ever seen horses cry before, and it was a terrible sight. He tried not to believe what those tears meant as he stood staring at his beautiful stallions. Then they broke the long primordial silence:

"Forgive us, dear master," said Xanthus. "We bring back to you Patroclus."

"Dead. . . ." said Balius. "We bring him dead."

Achilles did not weep. His face was like a rock. Very gently he lifted the battered body from the chariot and bore it into his tent, binding the latchets so that no one could enter. The stallions stood before the tent like watchdogs and let no one approach. Achilles remained alone with his grief all through the long twilight and the hours of night, and the next morning.

No one dared approach his tent and intrude upon his grief. The Greeks were afraid he might have fallen on his own sword, choosing to lie in death beside his comrade, but they did not dare approach.

"He will not kill himself," said Ulysses. "He has work to do first; he must avenge himself upon Hector. After that, perhaps . . . but not yet."

In the darkest hour of night Thetis arose from the sea and walked through the walls of Achilles' tent. He had not wept, but mothers can hear silent grief; she had heard his even in the depths of the sea, and had come to him. All night long he crouched in her embrace, not weeping, but making low hoarse whimpering sounds. She held his head to her breast as if he were a babe again, and stroked his face, and kissed him. Even in his terrible grief he was comforted by her sea-magic touch. He spoke only at dawn, just before she left him.

"Will you do something for me, mother?"

"Anything, son."

"Patroclus went to battle clad in my armor. The Trojans stripped him of it. It is worn by Hector now, that armor made by Hephaestus and given to my father as a wedding present. I mean to seek Hector out and combat him today, but I wish to appear in armor no less fine than that I lost, and to bear weapons no less fine than those taken from Patroclus when he fell. These can issue only from the smithy of the gods. Can you persuade Hephaestus to labor this morning and forge me new gear?"

"I have some influence over the lame god," said Thetis. "I was the one who nurtured him, you know, after Zeus had flung him from Olympus and he had fallen into the sea with shattered legs, helpless as a tadpole. I took him to my cave, mended his wounds, and raised him as my own child, giving him pebbles and seashells to make jewelry of, so that he grew clever in that craft. He will drop what he is doing and labor this morning. Weapons and armor more beautiful than those you lost will issue from his forge. By the time you are ready to combat Hector you will find what you need here in your tent. Now farewell, dear son."

On certain evenings the sun diving through clouds forges out the shape of armed men, taller than mountains, who burn in the western sky as if guarding the horizon. Their flaming delicate armor is what Hephaestus took as his model when he yielded to Thetis' plea and worked the morning through casting new weapons for Achilles. Like the red-hot sun-disk itself written over with a tracery of cloud was his shield. His spear was a polished volt-bright shaft that Zeus himself might have used as a lightning bolt. For helmet crest he sheared a plume of cloud-fleece and dipped it into the colors of the sunset.

When he gave Thetis this gorgeous gear, the tall nereid scooped up the little lame god, held him in her arms as if he were a child, and kissed him on the lips.

"Thank you, dear Hephaestus," she said. "Thank you for your kindness, for your quickness, and for your masterful craftsmanship. You are a great god now, Artificer-in-Chief for the whole flat world; your smithy is a volcano where you wreak implements for the high use of father Zeus and the Pantheon. God though you be, you shall always remain my own dear little tadpole, my sweet maimed foster-child, and from me you shall always have a mother's tenderness although I am cast in eternal flowing nymphhood and you in eternal middle age."

She kissed his seamed, charcoal-grimed face, set him down, and flew off with the glittering new armor made for Achilles.

THE SCROLL OF THE FATES

Every few years the gods were entitled to read in the great book of the Fates wherein was written all that had been and all that was to be. We use the word "book," but there were no books then as we know them. This tome of the Fates was a huge scroll hung from a place in the heavens beyond man's sight and written over with starry characters. Night-blue was this scroll, made from the dark blue hide of a heavenly beast, unknown to man, hunted by the gods once every thousand years in a great chase across the inlaid floor of heaven.

Night-blue was the scroll, and those winged crones who were the Fates, those twisted sisters whom even the gods fear, would dip their claws into starlight and scrawl their irrevocable decrees upon these dark pages. Once every several years the gods were summoned to read what was written on the scroll, to consider what they had read, and then to return to Olympus to conduct the affairs of men accordingly.

Usually the gods chose to keep man in ignorance of what was fated for him. Occasionally, though, when it amused them, or when they wished to seduce a mortal by special knowledge, or when coaxed by artful oracles, the gods would let slip some information in the form of a riddle. And it was this matter that the oracles uttered as prophecy.

These oracles tended to cluster in groups called "colleges," each of them dedicated to a special god. Apollo's priestesses were especially well-known. They dwelt in a huge cave dug into a mountain at a place called Delphi. It was volcano country. Through a fissure in the rock an aromatic steam arose from the very entrails of the earth. The priestesses set their stone tripods across this fissure, and squatted above it, breathing these fumes — which gave them visions. These visions, they claimed, were of the future. They also chewed laurel — which we know as bay leaf — which sharpened vision, or blurred it; whatever it is that makes a vision most real to those who have it. Their utterances were always couched in riddles, knotty ones; no one could understand what they were saying except other priestesses, who, for a fee, would interpret these riddles.

Now, prophecy about the Trojan war had made a rich tale from the very beginning. On this subject soothsayers blabbed the secrets of the gods without restraint. We have already met certain of these prophecies: The one which said the Greeks could win the war only with the help of Achilles; and the second part of it which said Achilles must die before Troy, but if he stayed at home and did not go to war he could live a long, peaceful life. We already know the choice he made, with the help of Ulysses. And Ulysses himself was the subject of a prophecy which said that if he went to Troy he could not return to Ithaca until twenty years had passed . . . and would return alone, beggared, unrecognized.

Now, on this day following the death of Patroclus, the gods were summoned again to the far reaches of heaven to read the great scroll. It was the first time since the war had begun that they had been so summoned, and there was much new matter to read in the flaming scrawl of the Fates. The gods returned to Olympus brimming with news, some chattering, others sunk in meditation. All were trying to think how they could best use this knowledge of the future to tease man into providing some special entertainment in the years that lay ahead.

They had three principal spokesmen to work through. Calchas and Chryseis were professional oracles. Chryseis, the Trojan, was a priest of Apollo. He was also father to Cressida. Calchas was the most influential among the Greek soothsayers. Sometimes he posed as a priest of Hera, at other times claimed the special confidence of Athena. Actually he freelanced, picking up clues from any god he could, and making pronouncements about what the Greeks should or should not do. When things were going well he was listened to with half an ear; when disaster struck his counsel was more valued. So, professionally, he was not quite averse to catastrophe.

But the one with the real heavy, fatal burning talent for the future was Cassandra. Bestowed upon her by Apollo was that most terrible of gifts — a *memory* of the future. And she kept her pronouncements rare because she knew how awful they were. However, she did not disturb the Trojan peace of mind at all. It will be remembered that Apollo punished her for refusing his amorous advances by capping his gift with a curse. His sentence was that although she would be able to prophesy with the utmost accuracy, and know that she was doing so, she would always be disbelieved by her own people.

Apollo came to her that night, sliding down one of the shafts of his sister's moonlight. He entered her chamber where she lay asleep. But she had trained herself never to sleep more than a few minutes at a time because her dreams were so terrible. She awoke now and gazed upon him where he stood igniting the shadows, and closing her eyes again, said: "You are so unwelcome a sight you *must* be a dream. It doesn't really matter. You have always ignored my need for privacy, and walked through the walls of sleep as though they were open doors. Speak, my lord. Why do you honor me with this visit?"

"To impart to you certain matter that I have read in the starry scroll of the Fates. There is much, much about Troy."

Apollo spoke at length. The last thing he told her excited her unbearably. She knelt before him and clasped his knees.

"Oh, great Phoebus — please, please, in this let me be believed. If he believes me, perchance he will take the opportunity to save his life, brave though he be. Please let him believe what I tell him. If you do so then I will put aside the loathing I feel for you, I swear I will. Somehow — I don't know how — I will school myself to respond to your love; but you must do this thing for me."

"Your idea of diplomacy, my child, will never cease to astound me. But make no rash vows. In the first place, you will be unable to keep them, lest they go against your inmost nature. Secondly, even if you could, I cannot break my vow, once given. This is a disability we gods suffer from. And that is why we so seldom make promises. Farewell, I shall visit you again. Try to restrain your impatience until that golden hour."

Chryseis found his daughter, Cressida, cutting flowers in the garden. He bustled up to her.

"A very important day, my dear," he cried. "Much business brews."

"How is that, father?"

She was picking roses. Her slender fingers plucked and snipped, moving like white moths among the petals. Her face was flushed, making the roses look pale. Their fragrance was all about her.

"I consulted the entrails of a pigeon this morning," he said. "A very informative set of guts. They told me that the high gods had been summoned by the Fates to read the great scroll. But there was no hint, no hint at all, of what they learned."

"Perhaps another pigeon is on the way with this information."

"No, no, the matter has not been published yet. That much I know. They're being very closemouthed, the gods. I resorted to other devices. Cast dice, juggled numbers, even tried a few eastern tricks with the conjunction of the stars. But no luck at all. The gods are silent, and I don't know what to think."

"Well, keep eavesdropping. Perhaps you'll hear something."

Girls in those days were very courteous to their fathers, even while being bored.

"It's absolutely essential that I learn something," Chryseis went on. "For the war has come to a most important pass. Prince Achilles will undoubtedly rejoin the fray. He will seek out Hector. And upon the Dardanian plain beneath our walls the two greatest heroes on all the flat world will fight until one of them is killed. Now it is upon such days that oracles grow rich. If I could pick up even the tiniest scrap of information, I would be able to prophesy to Prince Hector concerning the duel, and he would give me splendid gifts. Yes, so noble-hearted is he, this eldest and strongest son of Priam, that he would reward even a gloomy prognostication, and if, by chance, the forecast should be happy, who knows what treasures he might heap upon me?"

Just then Cressida saw him look past her shoulder and pin a greasy, fawning smile to his face. He made a deep bow. Cressida turned. She saw Princess Cassandra, who had entered the garden so silently it was if she had been made to appear by magic.

Cassandra saw the priest's daughter coming toward her with an armful of roses. They seemed to be little red flames. The girl was carrying a bouquet of fire. And Cassandra saw her in the midst of smoke and shrieks and falling timber offering a lover her corsage of flame. She spoke icily to quench the pain of the roses.

"Greetings, Cressida," she said. "I do not wish to interrupt your gardening. I have come to speak with your father."

132

Cressida watched her father with distaste. The man was practically jigging with pleasure and importance as he led Cassandra toward a garden seat.

"Priest," said Cassandra. "The gods last night consulted the scroll of Fate."

"I know, I know, good princess. So I have divined."

"Have you divined what they were told?"

"Unfortunately, no."

"Your patron, Apollo, has told you nothing?"

"Not a word, not a word. I am hopeful of persuading him by my arts. But it takes time, time. . . ."

"Well, I have been told. I know now the heavy oracles concerning Troy."

"Can you perhaps, dear Princess, find your way clear to confiding them in me?"

"No, I cannot."

"A pity. . . ."

"But I have not come to your garden empty-handed. I will give you a single piece of information. It concerns my brother, Hector. I tell you so that you may tell him. If I tell him, I shall of course be disbelieved."

"In all modesty, he will believe me," said Chryseis. "He knows that I — "

"Yes, yes. . . . Listen closely now. For this is a conditional prophecy. If he fights Achilles, he will be killed. But Achilles cannot outlive Hector more than three days."

"You say 'if.' Is it not ordained that they must fight?"

"Try to understand the way the gods entertain themselves, O oracle. There is always a margin of uncertainty injected into each edict concerning the future. That is the way the gods keep themselves in suspense about those affairs they themselves concoct, and make the spectacles more dramatic. This margin of uncertainty, this divine suspense, is called man's will — those decisions he makes about his own affairs. 'If,' my friend, is a tiny word of sublime proportions. If man properly taps the explosive strength of its pent possibilities he can alter circumstances, and thrust the gods themselves into entirely new situations. The word 'if' heads the prophecy. *If* Hector fights, he dies. *If* Achilles kills Hector, he too dies. Make this clear to Hector. He can avoid the fight. In all honor he can do so. No one else fights Achilles. Why should he? If he avoids this duel, he will live. Go. Tell. He will reward you. Here is a gold armlet set with rubies and sapphires to pay for the time you have given me. If Hector exercises his 'if,' and refuses to fight Achilles, then I shall add to this armlet a fat bag of gold."

Cassandra pulled the heavy gold circlet off her arm and gave it to Chryseis, who fell to his knees when he took it. The princess nodded to Cressida, and walked out of the garden.

As Cressida crouched again among the roses, Aphrodite now began tampering with affairs. She had come back from her session with the Fates teeming with mischief. Plan after plan for confounding the Greeks danced through her head.

"In my quiet way," she said to herself, "it seems to me I have been much more influential than those brawling hags, Hera and Athena. After all it was my gift of Helen to Paris that started this war. And who was it that embroiled Agamemnon and Achilles, instilling in them a desire for the same slave girl? And look what that has led to. Now, however, with Patroclus dead, Achilles is sure to take the field. When he does, that mighty sword will shear through the delicate web of my contrivances. What then? All is not lost. Achilles must slay Hector if they fight, says the scroll of the Fates, but if he does, he himself must die soon afterward. If he does not combat Hector, all is as before. If he does, and they both die, then a new situation prevails. Diomedes will be the most formidable hero in the Greek camp. And I have a sharp grudge against that bully, Diomedes. Did he not dare to raise his lance against me, me, the Goddess of Love and Desire, and wound me on the wrist? Wait . . . here's an idea! I can settle my grudge with him, and in doing so throw the Greek camp into turmoil again. All this, by heaven, without even making a new plan; I'll use the old one. As I once set Agamemnon against Achilles, now, should

134

Achilles die, I will set that Mycenean bull in murderous rivalry against Diomedes . . . and do it in the very same way — through Cressida, whom Agamemnon held as a slave, and whose ways intoxicated him. Now, I will infect Cressida with the sweet venom of love for Diomedes. She is already inclined that way, having watched him fight during his day of glory, and my job will be easy. Yes . . . I will raise admiration to a passion that will burn in her veins and melt her bones. And when she returns to Agamemnon's tent, nothing will keep her there. It is Diomedes she will want, Diomedes she will find her way to, hurling those two chieftains at each other's throats, dividing the Greeks into factions again, and weakening them altogether, so that they will be incapable of an assault against my Trojans."

Thereupon she took a vial of a thick gluey red ointment that smelled of honey and baking bread — the odor of desire. Invisible, she flew to the garden of Chryseis and smeared, with this venom of desire, the thorns of the roses that Cressida was picking. The thorns pricked Cressida's hands. Suddenly she burned for Diomedes and she knew that before the night had passed she must find a way to him.

"But will he want *me?*" she thought to herself. "He is in love with battle. Killing Trojans is his one passion. And murder is an absorbing business. Will it leave room for gentler occupations? Agamemnon I could twist around my finger. But for this Diomedes I feel a kind of terror. I must make myself irresistible to him. But how? By giving him what he wants the most. Yes . . . victory over the Trojans, that is what he wants the most. If I can bring him information that will help him achieve victory, then perhaps he will love me. Do I know any secrets? Nothing that is not generally known. Chitchat about the court, observations about the personal habits of Priam's sons and daughters — these will not be useful to him. No . . . I need something big, important. If, for only an hour, I could be that sour-faced Cassandra with her talent for reading the future, then I could come to him filled with the authority of an oracle,

135

a priestess of knowledge, and could make him love me. But that's it! Cassandra! Locked in her head is what I must know. I must unlock it. But how? She despises me. Whom does she not despise? Her brother, Troilus — that's who. She dotes on him. Watching on the wall, she has eyes only for his deeds, his safety. She would tell Troilus what I want to know. Then I must try to know Troilus a little better. It should not be difficult. He has a roving eye. It has rested on me occasionally."

And so, as we shall see, goddesses can be outwitted too. Or rather, can outwit themselves. For Aphrodite, attempting to confound the Greeks, had kindled a tiny flame that was to grow into a fire big enough to burn Troy even unto the last timber.

Chryseis visited Hector to tell him of Cassandra's prophecy, claiming it as his own. Hector interrupted him.

"If I had any doubts about fighting Achilles," said Hector, "I am quite rid of them now. I have always expected him to vanquish me. His pedigree is much finer than mine. He is not only the son of Thetis, queen of nereids, but great-grandson to Zeus himself. We lift our weapons against him in vain. With much pain we have learned that he cannot be hurt by spear-cast or sword-thrust. No arrow can wound him, no dart pierce his magically toughened hide. And in the use of weapons he has no equal. Yet, I have always known that I must challenge him one day, for I am the best we have, and we must counter their best with ours. To challenge him, to meet him, to pray for strength and skill somehow to pierce that invulnerable hide — to do this and then to die — this I have known to be my fate ever since Paris returned with Helen from Sparta. To meet him, to fall, and to account myself lucky to be spared the sight of Troy being sacked — that has been the best I could have hoped for. Now you tell me that my death must lead to his? And you call this a gloomy prophecy? My dear man, it is the best news I have heard in almost a decade. I just hope I can trust it. I don't take much stock in readings of the future, you know. We have

136

a prophetess in the family who claims to be divinely inspired, and she is invariably wrong. However, I shall do my best to believe what you tell me. Now I shall seek out Achilles with great joy. And joy strengthens a man's arm."

"Pray, prince Hector, consider — "

"Enough, good Chryseis. You have pleased me. Don't spoil it. Take this bag of gold, and go. And be sure to watch from the wall tomorrow. It should be an interesting afternoon."

THE
WRATH
OF ACHILLES

Achilles took the field. All aglitter he was in the new armor forged by Hephaestus. His shield burned like the sun-disk at dawn; his plumed crest burned with the colors of the sunset. Between dawn-colored shield and sunset crest his face burned white-hot as noon with pent fury. He leaped into his brass chariot and shouted to his horses. But instead of charging toward the enemy lines which they always did at the first sound of his war-shout, this time Xanthus and Balius tossed their heads, turned their long faces to him, rolling their great golden eyes.

"Pray, forgive us, master," said Xanthus. "But one word before you go into battle."

138

"It is this," said Balius. "Do not seek Hector in single combat. If you find him, you will kill him, for no one stands before you —"

"And if you kill him," said Xanthus, "you must die within three days, because that is the decree of the Fates."

"I cannot believe my ears," said Achilles. "When in the field no one questions my commands — from the lowliest Myrmidon to the most powerful member of the War Council — I am certainly not accustomed to consulting my chariot horses concerning tactics."

"It is for love of you we speak, dear master," said Xanthus. "Now do as you will."

"But one favor," said Balius. "Please leave instructions that we be burned on the same pyre as you. We do not wish to be driven by another master after your death."

"Noted," said Achilles. "Now be silent and obey orders. Forward!"

As Achilles took the field, Hector was being dressed for battle. Not by his squire, but by his wife, Andromache, who had begged him to let her prepare him for this day's fighting. He had hesitated. She had been present at the conversation with Chryseis and knew the prediction about his death. But she had not said a word to dissuade him from meeting Achilles. She had saved it all up, he was afraid, for this last hour before battle. And the one thing that could weaken him, he knew, was her weeping. But she had asked to be allowed to help with his armor and he could not refuse. And now she was dressing him in the gorgeous metal that he had taken from Patroclus.

"Dear husband," she said. "I am filled with such love and admiration that my hands tremble, and I can scarcely bind the latchets of your corselet. For in this heaven-forged armor you shine like the very morning star."

He looked at her in amazement. No tears, no reproaches, no mournful face. She was alight with love, brimming with serenity. Never since the beginning of the war had she exuded such

139

confidence. He did not question her, but accepted her mood with glad heart. He would have felt differently perhaps had he known how she had arrived at her present mood. But it was a secret he was never to learn.

The night before, Andromache had left Hector's bed. She wrapped herself in a dark cloak and made her way through the sleeping city. Mounting the inner steps to the wall and keeping to the deepest shadows, she avoided the sentry and climbed down the other side of the wall. There she crossed the Dardanian plain to a bend of the river called Scamander. Now she unwrapped her cloak, pulled her gown over her head and stood naked, white as a birch, in the moonlight. She stepped into the river up to her knees.

"River!" she called. "O tall brown god who loved me while I was yet a maid. River-god, strong brown lover, Axius, spirit of the Scamander, answer me now — for I have come to you once again."

The river was a blackness spangled with gold in the moonlight. And gold was the color of the god who arose before her.

"Many tender maidens bathe in my stream," he said. "Which one are you?"

"Andromache."

"Oh, yes? . . . I think I remember. Very sweet and willing. How have you been since last we met?"

"Flourishing, my lord. I am wife to Hector, son of Priam, first among the princes of Troy."

"Hector — the great warrior?"

"Yes."

"How long have you been wed?"

"Seven years."

"Why have you left his bed and come to seek me now?"

"Tomorrow Hector fights Achilles."

"Foolish child! Hurry home, wake him up, take him into your embrace! It is your last night together."

"No."

"No? Did you say it was Achilles he was fighting?"

"Yes."

"That's what I thought. My dear child, no one, no one at all, engages Achilles in single combat and returns to his wife. It's just not done. The man is completely fatal. Couching here on my river-bed I have watched him in action now for nine years and, believe me, he is the complete widow-maker. Go home and love your husband, lady; tomorrow you are a widow."

"I beg leave to differ," said Andromache. "There is something in woman that rebels against these ordinances of the Fates . . . these absolute iron edicts concerning the future. We do not like to foreclose on possibilities. To us the future is precisely that which is pregnant with new life, new chance, new luck. I have heard the prophecy concerning Hector, but I will not accept it. And I need an ally strong as Fate. That is why I have returned to you, O river-god."

"Strong as fate? You flatter me. More powerful gods than I bow to fate. I do well enough here, but after all I am only a small local deity. Beyond the banks of this river I have no authority whatever."

"Ahh — but rivers rise. Rivers rage. Rivers overflow their banks and extend their authority across great fields. They sweep away walls, cities. Rivers drink floods and grow to mighty torrents rivalling the sea. You are too modest, Axius. It is a new quality. I never noticed it before."

"And you are a very clever, very persuasive lady," said Axius. "Something I did notice before, but had forgotten. Speak plainly; what is it you want me to do? Ask me what you will, and if it is in my power I shall help you."

"Trojan meets Greek upon your bank tomorrow. Hector will meet Achilles on your shore. Go into flood, my lord. Rage over your banks — but selectively. Sweep Achilles away. Drown him in his heavy armor."

"How do you know they will fight upon my bank?"

"They shall. I promise."

"Then I promise to do what I can. Sweet Andromache, you have returned to me on a night of hot moonlight when I was feeling old and stagnant, and have restored to me the lusty tides of my youth. I will do as you ask though stronger gods oppose me."

Andromache returned to the palace and, later that morning, as she helped Hector on with his armor, she still gave off the fragrance of that river which half-girdled Troy, running from the mountains to the sea, with dragonflies blue as jewels darting at its ripples and with elm-tree and willow and tamarisk dipping toward their reflections. And yet it was a river which could change its temper with brutal suddenness — drinking rain, gulping floods from the hills, and rising, raging over its banks, devouring town and village.

And Hector, donning his shining armor, felt himself fill with the strength of that river whose presence had been brought into this room by his river-smelling wife.

Andromache spoke: "One request. You know I never meddle into your affairs. But do me this favor, my husband, my lord, and let me advise you out of a dream that came to me in the night."

"Speak, my dear."

"Do not seek Achilles beyond the Scamander, but stay within the bend of the river, and let him come to you. If you do so, according to my dream, you shall defeat the son of Peleus and win everlasting glory . . . and return to me after the battle is over."

She fell to the ground and hugged his knees.

"Promise!" she cried. "Promise, oh, husband, please promise!"

"I promise," he said.

A detachment of Trojans pretended to flee before Achilles and his Myrmidons, drawing them toward the Scamander. There they turned to face the Greeks within a half-circle of marshy land lying in a bend of the river. Achilles could not use his chariot; its wheels sank up to their hubs in the marshy ground. So he dismounted and fought on foot, followed closely

142

by his Myrmidons. But mounted or afoot he moved through the Trojan ranks like Death itself with his scythe. Every thrust of his spear drank blood. Charging ahead he broke the Trojan ranks, and the brown columns of his Myrmidons, festive as ants, gorged their swords on the flesh of the scattered foe.

Now Hector and his picked guard charged into the marshy arc in a flank attack on the Myrmidons. Howling with ferocious joy Achilles sought Hector through the mob of fighting men.

"Stand, son of Priam!" he roared. "Try your stolen armor against my weapon's edge! Stand and face me or my spear will find your life between your shoulderblades, and you shall die a shameful death!"

Despite himself Hector found his courage melting at the sound of that terrible voice. He did not turn and flee, but retreated slowly until his back was to the river and he could retreat no further.

"Now! Now!" shouted Achilles. "You have a narrow choice, killer of Patroclus. Death by water or death by blade." And he drew back to hurl his spear. But Axius arose invisibly from the depths of the river and cast a cloak of mist about Hector. Achilles, poising his mighty lance, saw Hector disappear. Saw mist rising from the bank of the river, hiding his foe from sight. He cast his spear into the column of mist, but saw it sail harmlessly through and land in the river. For Axius had lifted Hector in his arms and borne him safely to the other side of the river. And all Achilles could see was tatters of mist drifting across the face of the water, and he knew that Hector had escaped his wrath once again.

Now, in terrible fury at this loss, he turned upon the other Trojans, and killed, and killed, and killed. The wet marshland grew wetter yet with running blood. Men sank to the top of their shin-greaves. Only Achilles remained lightfooted as a demi-god, running over the surface of the mud like marsh-fire. His new-moon sword rose and fell as if he were mowing a field. Every time it fell, a Trojan died.

Finally, the Trojans in panic fled into the river. But Achilles followed with his Myrmidons and slaughtered them as they tried to cross the ford. Bodies fell into the river and disappeared. The water ran red as sunset. Now Axius arose again from the depths of the river — in his own form this time — and Achilles found himself confronting a figure tall as a tree with greenish, coppery skin.

"Halt, Achilles," he said in a voice that rumbled like a waterfall. "Son of Peleus, halt — before I drown you beneath fathoms of my outraged stream."

"You must be the god of this river," said Achilles. "Very well. I have no quarrel with you, my lord. My business is with Trojans."

"But I have a quarrel with you, you tiger in human form. How dare you stain my waters with blood? Pollute my stream with corpses? Prince of Phthia, you have offered me deadly insult, and now you yourself must die."

Axius leaned down scooping into the river with his mighty hands and flung a wave at Achilles. The heavy water hit him full, knocking him off his feet, tumbling over him. He fought for breath. Every time he tried to rise another wave knocked him down. The river-god stood waist-deep flinging torrents of water over the bank. Caught like a beetle in his heavy armor, unable to rise, Achilles was rolled over and over into the river itself. He must surely have drowned had not his mother been Thetis, daughter of Nereus, Old Man of the Sea, who bequeathed to all his descendants the power to breathe under water. But the Myrmidons had no such lineage; they were capable of drowning, and those that had followed Achilles into battle were caught in the rising waters and drowned, every one.

Achilles, who had stumbled to his feet, saw his men drowning about him, and could not help them. He sprang into the middle of the stream and challenged Axius, shouting: "Fight fair, you watery demon! I have contended with you in your element, and you have not killed me. Now come up on land and fight me with sword and spear."

But Axius uttered a cataract laugh and, knowing now he could not drown Achilles, tried to crush him under a weight of

144

water. He curled himself into a huge crested wave that towered taller than any building in Troy and smashed this entire mass of water down on Achilles, who was hurled to the bottom of the river. He felt himself being pummeled, beaten, choked — felt an unbearable pressure squeezing his ribs. His arms were crushed against his sides; he could not even raise his sword.

Seeing his enemy pinned helplessly to the river-bed, Axius now scooped up boulder after boulder and rained them down on the Greek hero — like a boy pelting the ground with stones, trying to squash an ant.

But Thetis, Lady of the Living Waters, knew everything that was happening in every sea and stream and river of which the earth drank. Rising swift as thought from the depths of the sea she appeared before Hephaestus, who worked at his smoky forge inside his volcano. Clasping him in her cool arms she flew the hot little lame god to the lips of the crater, and said: "Look! See what's happening! Axius is murdering my son!"

Hephaestus, blissful as a babe always at Thetis' touch, half-dazed before the sea-magic of her beauty, dived back into the volcano, returned with an armful of fire from his forge. Now this fire is hotter than man ever sees burning in any furnace. It is the essential flame, the very core of flame, burning deep in the bowels of the earth, and is the source of all flame. And the lame god cast this fire that was hotter than fire down upon the river-bank. It kindled reeds, elm-trees, willows, and heated the mud itself to a molten mass. The river boiled. Axius, god of the river, felt his flesh scorching. And while he was a god and could not die, he could feel pain, and the pain of Hephaestus' red fire was so terrible that he cried: "Hold, Hephaestus, hold! Hold off your red fire! And I will break my vow to Andromache and allow the son of Thetis to escape!"

The smith-god recalled his fire. Axius dived to the river-bottom to cool off his blistered shoulders. Achilles staggered to his feet, took off his helmet, emptied it of water, then clapped it on his head again, forded the river, and set off in chase of Hector.

Andromache, watching from the city wall, had been seized

with great joy when she saw the river rise. She was filled with a marvellous laughing happiness when she saw Axius hurl his crested wave and bury Achilles under tons of water. But when she saw the banks burst into flame, saw the river boil, and the river-god's hair burning, and heard his wailing — when she saw Achilles rise from the depths of the river like the spirit of vengeance itself, the terrible tin of his greaves cleaving the water, and saw him race over the plain seeking Hector, and the light flashing from his sun-disk shield and his new moon-sword — then she knew that in him was gathered the strength of a natural force, crushing all plots and stratagems and wifely schemes — then she knew that Hector was doomed.

"I will not watch him being killed," she said to herself. "I cannot bear it. No wife should be made to watch her husband being butchered. I will go back now and get my baby and, at the very moment that Hector falls, I will leap with my son in my arms, dashing out our lives on the plain below. Thus father, son, and wife will be burned on one pyre, and cheer each other on the last journey to Erebus."

She left the wall and went to her home. Entering the nursery she took her babe from the nurse's arms. But when she looked into its face her strength deserted her and she fell into a swoon.

Now, in the shadow of the wall, watched by his father and his mother and all the people of the court, Hector turned to face Achilles — breathing one last prayer as he did so:

"I call to you, Apollo. I ask not for victory, for victory cannot be given, it must be taken. All I ask is that my courage last; that my marrow does not freeze at his terrible war-shout; that my knees do not melt before the white-hot fury of his lipless face; that I can stand my ground before his dread charge, and meet him weapon upon weapon without fleeing. My father watches on the wall. The pride of Troy rides upon my shoulders. Fair Apollo, bright Phoebus, I pray you, let me face my death like a man."

Apollo heard and sent down a shaft of sunlight that hit the

back of Hector's neck, gilding his helmet and warming his courage so that he stood full to Achilles' charge. Met him sword upon sword and shield upon shield, standing firmly planted before that fearful rush that no other man had ever withstood.

But Achilles felt himself being caressed by a delicious chill. He was bathed in sweet combative airs. The clash of weapons was bright music to which he moved perfectly, as in a dance. And he was happy to have a partner for this deadly dance, happy that Hector did not break and run before him. He wanted to feast himself slowly and gluttonously on the death of the Trojan who had killed Patroclus. His new-moon sword flashed. It locked with Hector's sword. Intimately the blades writhed. A great shout went up from the walls of Troy as the people there saw their champion stand so stoutly against Achilles, parrying his thrusts, blade meeting blade in equal play.

"Can it be?" thought old Priam. "Will my long years be crowned by this enormous glory? Will my son really be able to stand against this monster?"

Achilles laughed aloud as he felt the force of Hector's parry.

"Well done," Achilles said. "You're as good a man as ever I met. Almost as good as the one you killed — but for that one you shall pay."

Hector did not answer. He saved his breath for fighting. He was putting all his strength into every parry and counterthrust, and so far had met sword with sword and had kept the terrible new-moon blade from shearing through his armor. But every stroke now that Achilles aimed seemed to fall from a great height, seemed to fall with greater and greater weight as if it were plunging toward the center of earth. Hector felt his arms grow weary, his shoulders numb with the weight of his own muscle bunching to move his arms. Achilles' blows fell with greater and greater weight, and the laughing voice grated in his ear.

"Not so soon," said Achilles. "Don't start to breathe so hard this early in the game, my fine Trojan. We have barely begun.

147

This is only a little early sword-play; the real work is still to come."

Then, with a magnificent intricate stroke that changed direction in midair, Achilles snared Hector's blade in his own, snapped the sword from the Trojan's hand and sent it flying. And a great groan went up from the watchers on the wall.

"No sword?" said Achilles. "A pity. It was my own sword, too, that you took from Patroclus. Never before has it been sent flying like this. But if you have lost your sword then you need no armor."

Now, coolly, relentlessly, he stepped around Hector, using his sword as delicately as though it were a small knife. And just as Hector had done to Patroclus, so did Achilles do now to Hector, shaming the Trojan hero by cutting the latchets of his armor. The breastplate fell off. The corselet fell away. The greaves were sheared away. And Hector stood naked except for his helmet.

But Hector, free of his armor, dodged away from Achilles' sword and ran for the city gate. Achilles flashed after him. Carrying full armor he still ran lightly as Hector did, cutting him off from the city gate and pursuing him around the walls. Like an eagle swooping upon a lamb was the armored Achilles, striding effortlessly after the naked Hector. Around and around three times did Achilles follow Hector — as Hecuba hid her eyes and Priam tore his beard and all the people lamented. Striding relentlessly after his naked prey, flashing in his armor like the evening star, Achilles pursued Hector around the city walls. And, after the third circuit, he lengthened his stride and caught him.

Now Hector fell into the burning embrace of that bright armor like a maiden who has run from her first suitor, but finally swoons into his arms. For Hector's wind was gone, his marrow was frozen, the hinges of his knees were melting with dread, and his manhood was run out. He fell into Achilles' bright embrace. One great hand seized Hector's hair and drew back his head, stretching the strong bronze throat like a lamb's to the knife. The other hand raised the new-moon sword.

And as Apollo shrieked in anger and threw a cloud across the face of the sun so that the entire Dardanian plain darkened, Achilles with a swift merciful stroke cut Hector's throat. Then, still unstained, unwearied, and bright as the evening star, he bound Hector's ankles with the embroidered girdle that Ajax had given Hector after their duel. He bound the other end of the girdle to the axle of his war-chariot, which had trundled up to him at his whistle. He leaped into his chariot, shouted to his stallions, and they began to gallop around the walls of Troy dragging Hector in the dust behind them. Seven times Achilles circled the walls of Troy, dragging Hector's body behind his chariot.

But Apollo threw a sleep upon Priam and Hecuba so that they would not see the body of their son being dragged in the dust. The sun-god also threw a magic balm upon the corpse of Hector so that the body was not broken or the flesh torn as it was dragged along the rough ground behind that terrible chariot.

With a final shout Achilles swerved his horses and headed back for the Greek camp still dragging the body of Hector.

'Could is should...
Should is would,
would is wood, of course.
What began with an apple
Must end with a horse.'

CRESSIDA

Late the next afternoon, while the armies were skirmishing on the plain, Cressida crossed the lines all unseen and entered the tent of Diomedes. She found a slave girl there heating water in a huge copper cauldron, a little pale girl whom Diomedes had captured in a raid two years before on the island of Tenos. The maidens of Tenos have squeaky voices and look like little white mice, but Diomedes had kept her as a bath-girl because her hands were so soft.

"Are you heating water for your master's bath?" asked Cressida.

"Yes, lady. He comes back all hot and grimy from the fighting. And blood-splattered — you have no idea! And he wants his bath immediately, and a cool drink, and fresh clothes."

150

"Heavy labor for so small a girl," said Cressida in her hoarse purring voice. "I am moved to pity. Now just disappear somewhere and I shall do your work this afternoon."

"Oh, no, lady!"

"Oh, yes, little girl."

"I daren't! I daren't! He likes things just so. He has to be scraped of battle-filth with this ivory stick. Then kneaded in every muscle with warm oil. Then anointed with cool scented oil. Then blotted with a fleecy towel."

"These are demanding tasks requiring enthusiasm and skill," said Cressida. "Nevertheless, I think I can do them passably well. So off with you!"

"No, lady, no! I cannot! I dare not! He allows no one else to bathe him. He likes the touch of my hands."

"You will be feeling the touch of my hands, little one, and you won't like the feel of them, I promise. Now get out before I lose my patience. And here are three pieces of silver for you."

"I will not take them; I will not go!"

Cressida slapped the girl across the face so hard that she knocked her off her feet. Then grasped her thin shoulders, pulled her up again, and shook her until her jaw wobbled. Seizing her by the hair she dragged her from the tent. Cressida held the little pale weeping girl in both hands and looked down at her through the tangle of her hair. The slave girl was like a white mouse in the clutch of a beautiful tawny cat.

"You will keep away from the tent all night," said Cressida. "Understand? If I catch a glimpse of your pasty face before morning I'll whip you till you can't walk. Hear me, little mouse?"

"Yes, lady. Anything you say."

"Here are three pieces of silver. Go find some soldier to kiss away your tears."

When Diomedes returned to his tent after the day's skirmishing he found Cressida there heating water in the big copper pot.

"Welcome, my lord," she said. "Did you have good sport today?"

He looked at her in amazement.

"Who are you?"

"Do you not remember me, O Diomedes? Many a time during the past months coming to Agamemnon's tent for a war council, you have found me there."

"Agamemnon's tent? Yes. But then you are the priest's daughter, the one that had to be returned to her father because Apollo shot arrows of plague into our camp."

"I did not ask to be returned to my father. It was his idea entirely. And now, you see, I have crossed over again. I have become attached to the Greeks — or, rather, to a Greek. To you, my lord. I have come back to you."

He looked her up and down very carefully, and said nothing.

"Let me help you off with your armor. Here is your cauldron all ready. Everything is ready: the ivory stick, the warm oil, the cool scented oil, the fleecy towel. I have acquainted myself with your bath habits."

"Where is my bath-slave?"

"Here I am."

"I mean the little girl from Tenos."

"I sent her away."

"You sent her away?"

"Do not blame her. She had no choice. I bribed her; she refused the bribe. I beat her. She could not refuse the beating. You will not see her until morning."

"But do you not know that you have richly earned a beating yourself for meddling with my servants?"

"I put myself into your hands, my lord. But why not let me take your armor off and bathe you? If you still want to beat me then I am at your disposal. But right now you must be weary."

"You are a daughter of the enemy," said Diomedes. "Your presence in our tents before brought disaster upon us. Cost us hundreds of men. How do I know that you have not returned with some treachery in view?"

152

"Oh, I have treachery in view," she said. "You are acute, my lord. I plan a massive betrayal — but of Trojans."

As she spoke she had been undoing the latchets of his breastplate. She drew off the heavy curved piece of bronze, and then began to untie the bindings of his corselet.

"After your bath, when you are rested, when you have been anointed in cool scented oils, and clothed in clean garments, and have drunk and fed, and your mind is unclouded by fatigue — then I will tell you what you most want to know."

Later that night when all the tents were dark, Cressida told what she had done.

"To make it brief, my lord," she began. "I come to you with those secret oracles which enwrap the fate of Troy. Things which must happen or be made to happen before you can storm those walls and sack the city."

"How did you come by such oracles? From your father, the priest? Forgive me, but I have seen him, my girl, and I do not believe he is the kind of man the gods really entrust their secrets to."

"Not from him. Of course not. But from Apollo himself — through Cassandra, whom the sun-god confides in even against her will."

"And she confided in you?"

"Not at all," said Cressida. "She loathes me. With good cause. No, it was her brother, Troilus, she confided in. For I, wanting to come to you, not wishing to come emptyhanded, resolved to bring you a love-gift you could not refuse. So I persuaded young Troilus. I asked the young prince to go to his sister, Cassandra, and make her tell him the oracles, and bring them to me."

"Why did Cassandra, who is so clever, and would know the importance of such oracles to the fate of Troy, why would she entrust them to anyone else?"

"She is clever, poor girl. But she dotes on Troilus, and can refuse him nothing — even as I dote on you. Besides, the poor thing is so accustomed to her prophecies being disbelieved that

153

she is eager to cast the future for anyone who pretends belief. And this I instructed Troilus to do."

"You are a very clever girl yourself."

"Love has sharpened my wits. Such love shows how stupid I am. And so cleverness can come from stupidity — which gives me hope I can tease some heat even out of your icy soul, King of Argos."

"The oracles!" cried Diomedes. "Tell me the oracles. What must we do to take Troy?"

"Two conditions are necessary. One of them is couched in a riddle. It says that Troy can finally fall only through an act of 'monumental piety.' And it caps this riddle with a verse:

> 'Could is should . .
> Should is would,
> would is wood, of course.
> What began with an apple
> Must end with a horse.' "

"Too much for me," said Diomedes. "Maybe Ulysses can figure it out. He has a head for such things. What's the other one? I hope it's a little plainer, or we'll be here for another ten years."

"The other one is quite plain, quite simple. It says Troy shall not be taken unless Troilus dies today."

"Today? Then it's too late! It is after midnight; the day has passed!"

"But before it passed, young Troilus had also passed — over the Styx into Erebus where he will join all his brothers sent before him by you and Achilles."

"You mean Troilus is dead?"

"I have had a very full day," said Cressida. "Here is a little souvenir of it."

She handed him a dagger.

"See, my lord, it is sharp. And it has been used. It is encrusted with that which should be more precious to you than jewels — the heart-blood of Troilus."

154

Diomedes leaped up. He was a brave man, among the bravest who ever lived, but now he was bathed in an icy sweat of horror.

"You killed him!" he cried. "He loved you, and you killed him! Why, you are Hecate's own handmaid, a witch out of hell."

"For shame," she crooned. "A warrior to be so shocked at the idea of death. How many men have you killed, my lord? How many beautiful sons have you butchered and left in the dust? Why begrudge me my one — which is my love-gift to you? How many times have you seen a cat who loves its master bringing him a dead bird or mouse to lay at his feet as a token of this love? So I lay Troilus at your splendid feet, my master, my king, my only love. His death is the key that unlocks the gates of Troy, and brings you victory — as soon as Ulysses reads the riddle of that other oracle."

"To kill an enemy in open warfare is one thing," said Diomedes. "But to slip a dagger into his back while telling him how much you love him is something else."

"Foolish man," murmured Cressida. "Your enemies die in pain and terror. Troilus died in bliss. My arms were about him, my lips on his. He did not even feel the blade. If so happy a death could come to all men, it would lose much of its unpopularity."

THE END OF THE WAR

This is how the prophecy was fulfilled concerning Achilles:

Priam came to Achilles' tent to beg that Hector's body be restored to him for honorable cremation. The old king humbled himself before the mighty youth — knelt at his feet, and kissed the terrible hands that had killed his son. Achilles relented, and promised to return the body. This kindness was to kill him. For when he bore the body to the city gate, Paris was hiding nearby. As Achilles lifted the corpse from his chariot, Paris loosed his arrow, which Apollo guided to the one vulnerable spot on Achilles — the great tendon behind the right heel. The arrow cut the tendon, killing him immediately.

The promise Achilles had made to his stallions was kept; they were burned on the same pyre, and never had to know another master's hands on their reins.

Ulysses, faced with the task of unriddling the oracle, prayed to Athena for wisdom. Whether she granted him new insight or refreshed his old cunning, he never knew.

"The verse ends with these words," he said to himself, " 'What began with an apple must end with a horse.' But what began with an apple? This war, of course. It was started by the golden apple of discord, which led to the squabble among the goddesses, to the judgment of Paris, to the abduction of Helen — all of which led to the thousand ships at Aulis and the siege of Troy. Then the war must end with a horse, the oracle says. What horse? What kind of horse? The verse tells, no doubt. Let's see now.

> 'Could is should
> Should is would,
> Would is wood, of course.
> What began with an apple
> Must end with a horse.'

"The answer is wood! A wooden horse! This is what the oracle clearly demands, leaving everything as murky as ever. What can we accomplish with a wooden horse? What do we want to accomplish? To get inside Troy, of course. Can we ride this wooden steed, jump it over the walls of Troy? Wooden horses are not noted for their speed and agility. Looking at it another way, it's not a horse but a statue. A statue? But yes. A statue to Poseidon, father of horses! That's it! A statue so big that armed men can hide in its belly and be obligingly rolled by the pious Trojans into Troy. That is what the oracle meant by 'a monumental act of piety.' It all fits."

Thereupon Ulysses set a gigantic plan afoot, the most cunning plot he had spun in all his artful career. On a beach hidden from the sight of the walls, he ordered carpenters to build an enormous wooden horse, varnishing it to a last luster, and ornamenting it with gilded mane and hooves. It was set on solid wooden wheels, and a trapdoor was cut into its belly big enough to hold twenty men.

Then Ulysses, Diomedes, Menelaus, Little Ajax, and sixteen other of their best warriors hid themselves in the belly of the horse. They wore no armor and carried no shields, lest the clanking metal betray them; they were armed only with swords and daggers. Then the ships were rolled down to the water, and launched. Masts were stepped, sails raised, and the fleet moved out of the harbor, behind a headland, out of sight. When they were hidden from view, they moored again to wait for a signal.

When the Trojans awoke the next morning, they saw no tents on the beach, no ships, no Greeks. The camp had disappeared. Even the cattle were gone, and the fires were cold. Rejoicing with loud shouts, weeping for joy, the entire population rushed out onto the beach. No one at all was to be seen. After ten years the beach was Trojan again — the war was over! It was unbelievable, yet unbearable to believe anything else.

They marvelled when they found the giant wooden horse, and tried to guess its purpose.

"Read what is written!" cried Chryseis.

Cut into the shoulder of the horse were these words: "An offering to Poseidon by the Greeks, who, after ten years of war, sail for home again, and beseech fair skies and following winds."

"Clearly, an offer to Poseidon," said Chryseis wisely. "And if we take it into the city and set it in our temple we shall be the ones to earn the favor of the Earth-shaker, who has been so hostile to us."

"Brilliant," said Priam. "The very thing."

"Fatal!" shrieked Cassandra. "That horse will devour Troy!" But no one heeded *her*.

Another of Priam's advisers, a man named Laocoön, had other ideas, too.

158

"Hear me, O king," he said. "Beware the Greeks, even bearing gifts. I mistrust this horse. I mistrust everything an enemy does. Let us take axes and chop it to pieces."

He was a very large, impressive, deep-voiced man. His words made Priam hesitate, and he might have convinced the king — but Poseidon took a hand. He sent two enormous sea serpents gliding up onto the beach. They seized the two small sons of Laocoön and began to swallow them whole. Laocoön leaped upon the serpents. But they simply looped their coils about him and crushed him to death as they finished swallowing his sons.

"Let the impious take heed!" cried Chryseis. "Those serpents were sent by Poseidon to punish the sacrilegious words of Laocoön. We must honor this wooden horse dedicated to the sea-god; bedeck it with flowers, take it into the city, and set it in our temple."

Awestruck by the fate of Laocoön, the Trojans did as Chryseis bid.

That night the fleet put into shore again. Under the command of Agamemnon the Greeks disembarked and waited on the beach. Exhausted by their rejoicing, the Trojans slept in their city. In the darkest hour of night, Ulysses crept out. Seeing no one, he tapped on the horse's belly. Diomedes and the others slipped silently out of the trapdoor. Menelaus dashed toward the palace and Helen, followed by half the men. Ulysses led the others to the wall where they surprised and killed the drowsy sentries — then set a signal fire on top of the wall, summoning the army. Ulysses descended and swung open the huge gates, and the main body of troops entered Troy.

The old tales go to great lengths now giving the names of Trojans slaughtered in the sack of the city and the manner of their deaths. But it is sufficient to say that the men were butchered, houses looted and burned, and, finally, the women and children borne off into slavery.

Of all the Trojan princes, Aeneas was the only one to escape

159

the massacre. Heedless of his own safety he lifted his old father, Anchises, to his shoulders, and carried him through the burning city. And the Greeks were so struck by his courage that they let him go.

He boarded a ship and sailed away into a series of strange adventures. After years of hardship and incredible danger he came to a fair land and founded a city later to be called Rome.

Cassandra was taken back to Mycenae as Agamemnon's slave. But she was murdered by his wife, Clytemnestra, on the same night that she knifed her husband in his bath. Cassandra had warned Agamemnon this would happen but he hadn't believed her.

Paris was presumed dead after the sack of Troy. But some say he fled, and lived under other names in other lands, protected always by Aphrodite.

Helen went back to Sparta with Menelaus and lived happily there as Queen. She explained to her husband that she had been abducted by force, kept in Troy against her will, and he chose to be convinced. She kept her beauty always and was much admired by the princes of Hellas who often found occasion to visit the royal palace in Sparta.

Cressida disappears from legend after the war. It is believed that she was taken to Argos by Diomedes, but what happened to her there nobody knows.

As for Ulysses, his real troubles began after he left Troy. It took him ten years to get back to Ithaca, and his adventures were so many and so marvellous they take another book to tell.

The flames that consumed Troy burned for seven years. They burned so hotly that the Scamander turned to steam and hissed away — and Poseidon himself retreated from their awful heat, shrinking his sea. Where the beautiful waters of Troy's harbor once flowed is now a parched and empty plain.